KIRKUS REVIEWS

TITLE INFORMATION

COMPANIONS?

Is It Asking Too Much?

Robert W. Spruce and Sherri C. Southers

BOOK REVIEW

A Roman Catholic discussion examines the male and female natures in the Christian faith.

The inspiration for the title of this book by Catholic Spiritual Directors Spruce and Southers is Genesis 2:18, when God saw that the man he created had no mate. The Lord then decided to create a woman to act as the man's companion and partner. The bulk of this brief work explores the nature of that relationship, between men and women and between men, women, and God. "When we believe that God loves us unconditionally and we believe that we want to…try to love Him in response," the authors write, "then it follows that we are now in the frame of being able to love others as Christ has loved us." In order to study things in general terms, the authors use overarching patterns. For certain aspects (positive and negative) of the male psyche and nature, they use the term "the Brutus Persona," and for the female personality, they invoke the Virgin Mary. The book's sections are introduced by bits of dialogue between the two authors as they expand on these ideas. "The Brutus male persona has serviced us well, if but brutally at times," Spruce contends, for instance. "Man cannot be as close to God as the woman because she is more like God than the male and is able to surrender, love, etc. to the man Jesus," asserts Southers at another point. This dialogue format often yields the work's most captivating sections. Many readers will wish there had been more dialogue and fewer digressions. At one point, Spruce maintains that "a man knows that a woman is different, but we don't really understand why. Sometimes women are too mysterious. We want women to be equal, but we don't want them to be men," to which Southers responds: "Good point." The authors take turns beginning these exchanges. This lively dynamic keeps the book moving forward.

A charged and intriguing exploration of gender differences through a Christian prism.

Companions?
Is it asking too much?

ROBERT W. SPRUCE
& SHERRI C. SOUTHERS

Companions? Is it asking too much?

Copyright © 2021 by Robert W. Spruce and Sherri C. Southers. All rights reserved.

No part of this publication may be reproduced, stored in a retrieval system or transmitted in any way by any means, electronic, mechanical, photocopy, recording or otherwise without the prior permission of the author except as provided by USA copyright law.

The opinions expressed by the author are not necessarily those of URLink Print and Media.

1603 Capitol Ave., Suite 310 Cheyenne, Wyoming USA 82001
1-888-980-6523 | admin@urlinkpublishing.com

URLink Print and Media is committed to excellence in the publishing industry.

Book design copyright © 2021 by URLink Print and Media. All rights reserved.

Published in the United States of America

Library of Congress Control Number: 2021900275
ISBN 978-1-64753-632-9 (Paperback)
ISBN 978-1-64753-633-6 (Digital)

24.11.20

We dedicate this book to those who are being sought by
God and who in return are seeking God. Finding God
and searching for God brings happiness, well-being and an
understanding of who we are in the eternity of God's economy.

We give thanks to those who have encouraged
and supported us through this project.

-Bob and Sherri

Table Of Contents

Introduction 9
In Conversation 13
Behold The Garden 15
- From The Garden.. 15
- Unconditional Love 17
- Love Thy Neighbor 21

Behold: The Man.. 27
- The Male Human.. 27
- The Brutus Persona 30

Behold: The Woman.. 44
- "This Is Flesh Of My Flesh" 44
- Bone Of My Bone..57
- The Female Response To Brutus................................61

Behold: "God's Gift Of Technology" 74

Behold: The New Person Man 82
- Jesus, "The Real Man"... 82
- The Male Persona Legacy 91
- Who Is This New Person Man (What God Had In Mind?)... 99

Behold: The New Person Woman 104

Behold: Am I A "Companion At Last?" 122
- Am I "A New Person"? 122
- Am I Self-Centered?... 126
- Can I Lose?.. 129
- Do I Think This Is Real?..132
- Am I Willing To Be A Companion During Conflict?........ 134

The Beginning Of Change 138
In Conversation 141
Appendix 143
Bibliography 149
References 153
About The Authors 155

INTRODUCTION

Our book is based upon topics of interest to Bob and Sherri. We began our purposeful spiritual conversations in 2009 with the idea of enhancing our own spiritual lives and deepening our own individual relationships with God the Father and the Son and the Holy Spirit. As our conversations deepened and our friendship and trust grew our conversations transformed from being focused on the "I" to being focused on the other (friends, family, acquaintances and the community at large) and finally to a curiosity in general of what are the key components of human relationships, communities and companionships. We are not experts in psychology, human relationships or theology; we are attentive observers and listeners and we are curious about the impact of human behavior, psychology, relationships and what one's concept of God has on the spiritual life of an individual person and on people in community.

We have integrated ideas and concepts from our first book *(A Journey of a New Person, Harden Not Your Heart)*, from our own observations, and from noticeable changes in society regarding human relationships and how these interactions impact our spiritual life in both discipline and longevity.

In our first book we explored the concept of becoming a new person. A new person is one who deeply desires to grow in their relationship with God and be transformed into His likeness. The new person diligently works with themselves and others and God to persevere in the spiritual life moving toward God in all areas of life. We strongly believe in the concept that we must become "new persons" in order to be in the types of relationships that God intended for us to engage in with Him, ourselves and our neighbors. As Catholic Certified Spiritual Directors we individually strive to be new persons and we listen to others in their struggles on becoming new persons as well as listening to their desire to deepen their relationship with God. As individuals progress in their relationship with God, there are subtle transformations that are noticeable. When the individuals become new persons they blossom into relationships of men and women and these interactions challenge them both individually and as a couple. How do the opposite genders impact their mutual relationship, either negatively or positively, as they each continue their journey to understand themselves and others?

We simply explore and discuss what it means to be a new person, the benefits of persevering in becoming a new person, the challenges in becoming a new person, how becoming a new person transforms the heart, relationships, communities and companionships. All this in the backdrop of how we think God meant for human relationships to be along with the powerful impact of God's attitude of loving our neighbor which transforms individuals, relationships, companionships, and communities.

We began with the question of how does male domination impact our society and our relationships? We discussed and researched male domination, the basic characteristics of men, and why males seem to be so linearly focused. We have found that through natural circumstances we are living with the legacy of a male dominated world.

Women and men are equal in the eyes of God but different for a purpose. The foundation and primary consideration of our conversations is how has male domination impacted our society and our relationships. We propose that the character persona in which most males live is neither "who they really are" nor any longer appropriate nor required and actually hinders the development of all civilization. These characteristics keep male humans from knowing and embracing the world, and their psyche.

We suggest that men have wonderful God-given characteristics that have propelled us to today and yet some have been distorted to serve distorted self-centered desires. We suggest that changes need to be made and that his helpmate is the woman who God generously gave to him.

IN CONVERSATION

Sherri: *"We have had many conversations over the years concerning relationships, and particularly how those between men and women play out in the world. It is interesting to us how these relationships work among those considered to be "new persons", i.e., those who through free will are seeking God in their lives and who are responding to God's pursuit of them." So, Bob maybe we could share some of our observations with others. (Reference our book: A Journey of a New Person, Harden Not Your Heart)"*

Bob: "Yes, and it has been a very interesting journey for both of us! We have made several observations through our research/reading/discussions that natural circumstances have us living the legacy of a male dominated world."

Sherri: *"And, we have grown to understand that men and women are different in many ways. Women and men are equal in the eyes of God but different for a purpose!"*

Bob: "Yes, and God has made them different for that purpose. We believe that male dominance must now realize and appreciate these differences! We had to be a certain type of male to respond to our might-makes-right environment. However, aspects of this male persona are no longer of value and were never very compatible with the female. But things are changing. God's universe is now different and will continue to evolve differently in terms of relations. For men and women to do God's will, i.e. be the "companions" God meant for us to be, we must change the nature of our relationships with one another. This will take work on both sides, changing the male persona and changing the way the female responds to him."

Sherri: *"Yes, let's look at the interactions between men and women with these three topics at the forefront; relationship, community and companionship. Let's explore and discuss what it means to be transformed into a new person all in the backdrop of how we think God meant for human relationships to be along with the powerful impact of God's attitude of loving our neighbor and focusing on what God is asking of us. The time has finally come to do His will, to be companions!" But is it asking too much?"*

Bob: "Sherri. Let's ask our readers to take a trip with us and to consider their answer to the following question. *Are you willing to consider looking at yourself to determine if you are a new person companion in your relationships?* Our desire on this journey is to help us understand how we are doing as we try to accomplish God's will in our lives, relationships, communities and companionships. And do we think it is doable or is it asking too much?"

BEHOLD THE GARDEN

FROM THE GARDEN

Scripture speaks of the woman as being created with the man, "in the divine image of God", equal but different than the man, but "flesh of his flesh" and "bone of his bone". The words "helper", "partner", "companion", and the phrases, "the woman you gave to be with me", "the woman whom you put here with me" all speak of something more than just the propagation of the species.

A "companion" is a word that may best speak of this relationship in the way God created it to be. A companion accompanies another, associates with them, assists them, is a mate or a match to them. Since the woman came from the rib of the man they were once the very same person. The resulting child from reproduction was a child with both of their DNA's – taking companionship to the highest level in the creation of a new being.

There is no definition of a despotic hierarchy implied because both are with and help one another in a hierarchy which is benevolent. To be a helper is to give assistance or support to another implying that the other needs to have the helper to be who they must be. Woman was created to reveal to man more of God's love and life. She was designed to fulfill his wishes, to quell his yearnings, and to give full weight to his human existence by being human with him, coming from him and therefore knowing him from the beginning.

The Catechism of the Catholic Church (CCC) articles 369, 1605, and 1609 speak of the woman as representing God from whom all wisdom comes, our helper. Though different physically and psychologically women are the helpers required to understand the world and to make right decisions about many things. Even depth psychology as it views personality from a dynamic and unconscious motivation sees this in the necessity of each of us having a subconscious that has a male and a female presence and how if we are to be healthy these need not ever reach the extreme of either. This keeps our individual sexuality paramount as it should be but also blends male and female together individually in such a way that, united as one, we act as one in a healthy way as true companions. That is why God made us equal with equal dignity in the image of God and to be better than we are individually.

Yet in a world that was based around a "might-makes-right" structure that gave power to the strongest, enjoyment of this intended union with equality was made difficult. Though God made everything, including man and woman "good" he also gave us free will as a sign of real love and as a way of showing or rejecting our love for Him. We of course recall that as man matured through evolution there came a time when he could differentiate right from wrong. And in many ways in defiance of God's will many chose to use this free will for evil instead of good. Thus, we have the Fall in the Garden and the "Flood" to help us understand what could happen when we choose to do evil instead of good, i.e., to sin.

FROM THE GARDEN

UNCONDITIONAL LOVE

The concept and definition of love is huge. For our purposes we are using the following definitions and explanations of love for our discussion. Our focus is the unconditional love God has for His people.

Love is patient, love is kind. It is not jealous, love is not pompous, it is not inflated, it is not rude, it does not seek its own interests, it is not quick-tempered, it does not brood over injury, it does not rejoice over wrongdoing but rejoices with the truth. It bears all things, believes all things, hopes all things, endures all things. Love never fails. So, faith, hope, love remain, these three: but the greatest of these is love. *(NAB 1 Corinthians 13:4-8, 13)*

"God is Love" *(1 John 4:8,16)* **and His love is unconditional and His love for us is His first gift containing all others. "God's love has been poured into our hearts through the Holy Spirit who has been given to us."** *(Romans 5:5) (CCC 733)*

Love may be defined as when we attach ourselves to an object such as God which is presented by the intellect as good. It manifests itself in attentiveness care for the other's welfare, delight in their presence and the desire for their approval. It resides in the rational will and, also in our sensory faculties. The two wills become one spirit. There is no fear of inequality of the two parties. *(A Catholic Dictionary, Donald Attwater)*

Unconditional love is the paramount key that opens the door to one's proper relationship with God, one's self, one's neighbor and His creation in general. The ultimate of this is the happiness that comes through the relationship of "companionship" that we will discuss as we move through the thought progression of this book.

What does, "God loves me unconditionally" mean? God loves me, period! There are no conditions in which He does not love me. No matter what I may have done in the past, no matter what I am doing at this moment, no matter what I might do in the future, God loves me without any conditions. He loves me. He forgives me when my heart turns away from His love, for sin sets me against His love for me (CCC 1850). When I confess my sin, I am forgiven through Jesus, the Christ. He only wishes for me to spend eternity with Him. God compares me with no one. He takes me and deals with me on my own. He judges me as a loving father judges a child for, I am one of His children.

So, am I off the hook and able to do whatever I wish to do without ramifications from this God who loves me unconditionally? "NO".

When I can truly say that I believe God loves me unconditionally then I have crossed over from a God of judgement and condemnation who I physically fear to a God of love and a God that I love in response to His love. It is my true belief that allows me to want to respond to God with love always. Am I able to respond to God with love always? "NO". But I want to, and I try to despite the quality of my effort, despite the success of my effort. I WANT TO: I TRY! I TRY! I TRY! because I love God in response to His unconditional love for me.

But to love God I must also be transparent with God. He is all around me, all the time. He sees all and knows all. As the Psalms (Psalm 139) remind us, we cannot get away from God's presence. But only in his constant presence can we be who and what we were meant by Him to be. Therefore, when I sin and I know when I do, I ask Him to forgive me and I TRY to do better. He forgives me. End of that particular "sin story". He expects me to be open, to talk to Him as a friend, in this case a friend who can always be trusted and never leaves me alone.

For all of us this mutual love relationship between God and man (ourselves) means that through conversion we must open ourselves to a new way of responding to God, ourselves and our neighbors. We are all called to have a God-based relationship, be it in community and in our most personal relationships, and companionships. We are called to be our real selves which allows us to remove any false personas that inhibits this conversion.

A part of knowing in my gut that God loves me unconditionally is believing that I want Him to have control of my life. This does not mean I give up my ego, my personhood. It means that I know He will always do what is best for me in the context of myself in eternity. Because I was made to be His child, I try always to do His will as the meaning of my life and existence. I am to be open to Him, to try to hear and understand His will for my life. I talk to Him, and listen to Him and believe I hear Him, through prayer!

If God loves me unconditionally, then I must love myself unconditionally. This is a hard saying! I know me too well and for some reason I may find it hard for me to love myself unconditionally. But if God loves me unconditionally then is it blasphemous for me not to love myself unconditionally? I must try to do right in the eyes of God, but the emphasis is on try, not attainment of perfection. Only God is perfect. I am not. If I think of myself as perfect, I would be committing blasphemy since only God is perfect. But I am expected to "try to be more perfect" and ask God for forgiveness. We are told that a more accurate translation of "perfect" in the New Testament is "to be whole". To be whole before God is to love and be honest in His presence, even when we fail.

So, if one believes that God loves one unconditionally, then it also means that one accepts who they are despite their regrets and imperfections. We are who God created us to be. Remember, the words "assumption", "comparison" and "judgement" should not exist in the language of the Christian. Only God has the ability to know how these words apply to us. God does not compare us with other human beings, nor should we. We should be thankful for being who we are and believe that God's mercy and control in our lives will be of benefit to us.

"Love is a paradox. It often involves making a clear decision, but at its heart, it is not a matter of mind or willpower, but a flow of energy willingly allowed and exchanged, without requiring payment in return." *(The Universal Christ, Richard Rohr)*

FROM THE GARDEN

LOVE THY NEIGHBOR

Once one feels in their gut that God loves them unconditionally and accepts that He loves them unconditionally then the application of loving God, self, and neighbor fosters harmony in God's creation and within the person. For many the phrase, "God loves me unconditionally", may be hard to believe at all, let alone believed in one's gut, i.e., personally accepted and believed completely and truthfully. There may be a feeling that, "I should feel this to be true". But often this is not truly believed because of what was instilled in our minds during our maturing from childhood, our particular Christian denomination's view of God or what we perceive to be our own moral failures either in thought and/or in action. Nor is this necessarily a sudden realization due to a conversion experience or a "public acclamation" of Jesus Christ in our lives. For many this is a slow realization of who God really is, i.e., a God of infinite love and kindness. One may not remember the exact moment that this truth is received as a gut belief but the feeling at some point becomes different. "I believe in my gut that God loves me unconditionally".

When we believe that God loves us unconditionally and we believe that we want to and try to love Him in response then it follows that we are now in the frame of being able to love others as Christ has loved us. This means that we are able to love and can try to love our neighbor as Christ loved us and as we love ourselves.

We too can now love unconditionally. What does that mean? We can look at others unconditionally and non-dualistically, i.e., without our conditions only and without the human person being viewed in everything as if there are only two opposing options. Yes, it's true that all may not feel as we do about God and may not even believe that God would ever love us unconditionally. No matter, what the other is like or thinks, or feels, we as God's children love others despite themselves. We can give them the benefit of the doubt unless we learn, the emphasis here on learn, that we cannot. Assumptions are often wrong and do harm. We need to at least be willing to change assumptions in the face of reality. Our goal is to consistently act in the context of the 20/80 rule, the paradox to the 80/20 rule in which we keep a healthy ego by thinking of ourselves 20% of the time but thinking of others 80% of the time as well suggested by, "loving our neighbor as ourselves".

God loves us unconditionally, why cannot we love the other unconditionally? With our eyes wide open we love others as ourselves, i.e. unconditionally. Yes, there is evil, and men create evil because they do not believe that God loves them unconditionally. But until we can identify evil in another, we must try to assume good and that God is in all. We must practice mercy, empathy and forgiveness, and exercise charitable interpretation thus learning to, "live in the Mind of Christ".

Our loving someone unconditionally gives us insight into how God loves us unconditionally and what it means for us to love another unconditionally. Loving others unconditionally is not easy, and it takes practice and discipline and it is a choice we have made as new persons to imitate Jesus. Others may treat me however they want to treat me, good or bad or indifferent, and my choice is to continue to love them anyway. They do not have to love me in the same way they love their friends but for me I still choose to love them unconditionally. They might need at times to take the first step in reconciling with a friend in order to repair the relationship, but they do not have to take that first step with me in repairing our relationship because I love them unconditionally anyway. This is how God loves us! He always reconciles the relationship we have with Him. If we attempt to imitate Him, we must practice His ways.

We may annoy God with our lack of love for Him or others, we may seem oblivious to Him, we may not deliver in the best way in our apostolate, we may do things that are traditional sins in the eyes of God and be fully aware of it. Yet, we are forgiven by Him unconditionally. If we love another person unconditionally then we can do the same.

We can even love our Neighbor in our most Intimate Relationship

"And by the way our spouse is our neighbor."

Our English word love can be a source of confusion. As we must remind ourselves love relationships can be quite different and especially love in its romantic way is not always the way Hollywood portrays it. In a lot of ways this approach to romantic love may be confused with the broader definition of the word. Romantic love superseded reality after the Middle Ages leaving us with the belief that Knights in Shining Armor and Ladies-in-Waiting and chivalry were the icons representing love between a man and a woman. We have been somewhat misled, and we might think the fantasy is reality which it is not. The fantasy may be our personal egos and actions instead of the true love of openness, trust, friendship and companionship shown in romantic as well as in other meanings of love.

If we believe that true love and companionship between a woman and a man is based on looks, money spent on rings and weddings and honeymoons and if these criteria insure, a life-long future of companionship then we may be in for trouble and many are already there. The "prince charming" and "daddy's little princess" are throwbacks to a day that never existed.

Romantic love in the past between a woman and a man does not coincide with the way we think about it today; in reality it was no more than a forged contractual relationship being more economically based and politically strategic even at the lower levels of society than heart and friendship based. Relationships in the way that fosters companionship rarely existed and rarely were the criteria for forging marriages. These were the dreamed plots of poems and stories but were too often not real life. We suggest that even less occurring was a friendship/companionship that evolved into a contracted marriage. But reality again, …… to not be married for either was not accepted! To be a "her" and not married was dangerous in all ways!

In some regards in today's world there have been changes to mitigate the "single" element danger. However, when it comes to those in marriage contracts maybe we have not fared much better than those before us going all the way back to the ladies and the knights. Are we now tying the once eternal knot because we are in relationship: attracted to one-another, close friends and companions who open our hearts and ourselves, to one another? Or do we still do it the old fashion way? …..what makes me look good?……good to family, society, our own egos, our need for nesting, our economies, our need to be contractual before all. We suggest that this is too often the case. And oh, by the way, where is God? He did not even really make the list! God should be at the start of the list if we really want a relationship that is real and endures through all the hell and all the heaven on earth that love gives a woman and a man.

Let's look at what goes on today between women and men, why it often does not work well even in the long run and why our divorce rate shows that the relationships meant to be are not.

To really be the knight and the lady of the myth in our relationships we must often make major changes to our attitude in caring for one another. There is no question that love between humans is one of the absolute realities of human nature. Love, even if stuck in the knight/

lady myth in a nagging way, knows that love is not simply a state of "doing" it is also a state of "being", "a relatedness, a connectedness to another mortal, an identification with her or him that simply flows within me and through me, independent of my intentions or my efforts." This gets things going!

What gets in the way of this beautiful natural flow is the ego which is a doer and is self-centered. Self-centeredness as we have seen keeps us enthralled with our selves thinking of ourselves 80-100% of the time and maybe other(s) at best 20% of the time. It's hard to see the trees for the forest and the forest is the "other". Often, this self-obsession is not who we really are but maybe who we have been made/taught/molded to be by others and society.

But love goes beyond ego, maybe at least 20/80 instead of 80/20. Love is real and the self-loving ego is not. Love is really what I am deep inside. Love is the power within us that affirms and values another being as he or she is because this gives value to each of us.

IN CONVERSATION

Sherri: *"At this point we have only scratched the surface of our discussion. Our discussion continues in the following chapters where we divide the discussion into the topics of men and women and what is underneath our exterior personas. We explore the interior view men and women have of themselves and of each other. The chapters explore the possible reasons why it is difficult to love one another the way we desire to love and the way we desire to be loved. We discuss what is within us that keeps us from being a new person God intended, why we struggle too in our relationships, communities, and in our companionships."*

Bob: "Good point Sherri, I think that would help facilitate our conversation by talking about some of the differences between the genders."

BEHOLD: THE MAN

"BRUTUS"

THE MALE HUMAN

The male human is the dominant living entity of our planet. He has been since the beginning of his existence. It is due to his dominion that the human race has survived. That dominance saved the human species for millenniums negotiating at best a human and animal "might-makes-right" world of dualism requiring often the immediate response of violence for survival. Whether intuitively or by a form of evolution the male psyche developed into an immediate response to the environment around him; a necessity to protect himself and provide for those physically closest to him.

Along with this immediate response developed other characteristics to enable the male living in the might-makes-right world to survive, prosper and dominate. Among those characteristics were incorporated an intense self-centeredness based upon an egotistical orientation. His physical and mental superiority over other animals, his very narrow focus of purview of all things in his environment, his single-mindedness and his necessity to control made him opinionated as to his superior role in the world and created the mind-set of a leader, protector of his own, jealous and possessive of his own, sexually potent, and abandoning of whatever got in the way. This created his narrow view of his dangerous environment and made his dualism seemingly apply to everything often in a zero/sum game approach to life. His ego produced an immediate response acted out in a dualistic way. For example: a man in the woods facing a ten-foot grizzly bear with a spear has no time to contemplate, he must react quickly to ensure his survival and that of any others.

This developed into the male affinity for the hierarchical. His self-centeredness and ego forged a propensity for all relationships to be competitive in nature and the necessity for a one-on-one mentality over all other males. His dominance of all others meant dominance of all others, other men, women, and beasts in order to keep his position of hierarchy and preserve his place of honored importance.

He relied on the fruits of dualist logic that resulted in violence. Therefore, for his survival or his clan's he had a strong propensity for war which went well with his need to "fix" things and to reap where he did not sow if required.

He carried this over into societal organization with a dualistic approach to all in his environment based upon logic, order and retribution. He defined and executed justice. He was authoritarian and prejudiced based upon his view and those who benefited from his authoritarianism.

And he did what he wanted by being stoic in nature and disposition. He must wear the false self of non-emotion with guarded feelings and guarded emotions. He must suppress emotions to the point of hiding his true feelings that are so buried in his persona that he more easily disregards them in his conscious thought. In short, he must be willing to subordinate all other emotions that do not make him dominant over other men. He must be morally disengaged if expedient and have a hardened heart toward such emotions as compassion, mercy, forgiveness and any concept of nurturing. This is the dominance within him of his head over the heart seen in his need to solve problems immediately and "fix things" at all cost.

But this psychological isolation takes its toll because he too is human and therefore in relationship with others. Therefore, the male is often a moody and a lonely person. And these have to a great degree been the characteristics of all males. This is "him", then and now. He has become this by the necessity of survival in the might-makes-right world. He must be this persona in his relations with all!

In review we are suggesting that all males have some of these characteristics within them:

- Self-centered and egotistical.
- Generally, has a narrow purview of his environment and everything in it and is dualistic in his personal view of that environment.
- Prone to violence in resolving issues of all types be they physical, emotional or personal.
- Prefers a hierarchical system so that he is secure in his position in all areas of life.
- Accustomed to suppressing his emotions with a hardened heart toward compassion, mercy, forgiveness, and the concept of nurturing.
- Often moody and feels lonely and unhappy interiorly and this can never be shown exteriorly.

We propose that this persona in which most males live is neither "who they really are" nor any longer appropriate nor required and hinders the development of all civilization. These characteristics keep male humans from knowing and embracing the world and their psyche.

BEHOLD: THE MAN

"BRUTUS"

THE BRUTUS PERSONA

The characteristics we just reviewed are those of what we have decided to call the Brutus persona which we maintain has existed now in various similarities for thousands of years and is the basic make up of most of the current male population. Having to react repeatedly and quickly to environmental challenges has created the man of today who has been trained by evolution to think dualistically and quickly. Whether hunting or protecting or war or in the executive office the man has to react immediately in order to survive and provide and protect. He has little to no time to evaluate and discern his actions. He might have planned a hunt or a battle, but the battle typically had too many variables and he had no control nor prediction of the outcome. In order to make these quick potentially fatal decisions he had to lessen the number of man-related variables that he had to discern in order to act. The evolved answer was to develop characteristics that could be molded and repetitive no matter what the dangerous situation might be. These characteristics had to be taught or learned by all males in some way and had to be handed down by males and their supporting mates from generation to generation. In no way could any of these characteristics involve time and/or emotion. They had to be preprogrammed into the man's psyche and into his physicality.

So, the man we see acts swiftly and decisively as does Brutus. He needed to be able to discern quickly many different options and he needed to give instinct to many other options. For example, he had to be narrow in physical and mental focus and dualistic in reaction, i.e., yes or no, good or bad, right or wrong, act or not act. His response dualistically had to be based upon what he had been taught by his society and experience. It generally had to be almost immediately decidable. He had to be extremely egotistical and self-centered, knowing what was in his own personal as well as his own personal peripheral interests that he had to protect. His motivation had to be clear! He had to be extremely competitive since losing was often a zero/sum game.

To protect himself even within his own clan, he had to be competitive and be "one up" on those in his clan in order to take care of his own interests. Hierarchy became the organizational norm based upon might-makes-right. Hierarchy told him who he was in society and where he belonged in the society as well as where he was to be in a battle. Practically, with so many elements of conflict he had to completely understand what was expected of just him. He had to defer other areas of the battle to others. His complete narrow focus had to be oriented to his specific function at that specific moment.

Emotions and feelings had to be guarded and not revealed or he was weakened. Response to emotions takes too long to digest and therefore must be removed from consideration by removing it from thought. A man had to be stoic and have a domineering attitude toward others in order to control his emotions which unless aggressive enhancing could not be outwardly shown. Compassion for the other was not the rule since you win, or you lose all. Weakness means you lose, and you do not deserve compassion. In a way this was even true in relation to his compatriots who had the same conflict functions. Even in instances where conflict involved a group of men with the same objective and working together to either succeed or fail, the individual's contribution was still the focus. Surrendering by men in any way is often very difficult. Men are expected to win no matter the odds. Life to many men was a zero/sum game then as it is today.

This Brutus had all these characteristics wired, cocked and loaded, ready to react. Reaction, not contemplation, was ready with any dependence on discernment to be short.

Physically and from a reactive psychological standpoint the Brutus persona, was ready and had to be worn by all. But the Brutus persona, in reality, was false, a mask covering who the man really was. It worked outwardly in dealing with the environment and was acceptable by all as the persona needed to provide, protect, and propagate.

The reality was that the persona was psychologically at odds with the real person male. He was not whom he claimed to be. He probably felt it then as men do today but was confounded by it and just accepted, "that is the way it is". But everyone had grown to accept and expect Brutus. It worked! A man was graded on his "Brutus" quotient".

Along with these male characteristics that were needed to survive other sociological factors contributed. All groups and more formal organizations were based on the might-makes-right that implies a hierarchical order and for most structures that resembles the structure needed for combat. Men agree to be dominated by other men in hierarchical systems. But hierarchy is tenuous. The underlying assumption of his competition characteristic is that the one on top is always in a tenuous position that can be unseated by another male. Things are never assured.

In history he was tempered by this curse by Christianity in the First Century and through the psychological illusion of romanticism arising in the Middle Ages. In reference to Christianity in the First Century and the Brutus male, we are challenged by what Jesus and the Apostles teach versus how the Brutus male persona has played out over the last two thousand years. Christianity in dogma and in practice is certainly the acute opposite of the might-makes-right personal self-centered nature of the Roman empire in which the value of individuals is compromised and devalued – the great example of man thinking himself to be able to be God! The pre-Constantine Roman empire being just the opposite of Christianity.

Even though Christianity made inroads into the psyche of the empire and individuals the world remained a "might-makes-right" world of Brutus male characteristics/male dominance. But the transformation began in our Gentile view of the Trinity, of the value of a person and relationships, the idea of spiritual community and the eternal view of God's victory over sin and death. All this with a slow evolutionary beginning in a change of men, women and companionship. However, the seed was sewn, the flower in the form of Mary, Mother of God who would eventually change our view of companionship between women and men. (Mary plays a key role that is associated with women that will be discussed later.)

In order to maintain the Brutus persona, the male had to apply his male characteristics to his environment. Therefore, his dominative role and characteristics made him mentally view the environment, creation, other humans, especially men and women close to him as "use items" that are there only to further his own self-centeredness and competitiveness. These use items had to be conquered. In his mind this was his will and the "will of God/the gods".

The environment must be conquered and placed under his dominion through science, engineering, art, invention and with it of course there must be a philosophy that explains it all and says that he is doing what he was meant to do and that he is, "right". As the Christian world of fact and mysticism in the Middle Ages is attacked, kidnapped and slid into moral depravity by the Reformation and the Enlightenment we see Brutus's ego replacing the Church as the foundation of moral acceptance and guidance. This only intensifies the Brutus male's persona and its false self. He, through a misguided understanding of philosophy, science, freedom and rationalism replaces God with himself believing that he, unto himself has the ability to define all aspects of his environment. "Behold the Man" who no longer needs

God and surely not God directly in his life and no longer needs the Church as Christ on Earth!

The Brutus male persona works so easily in this post-Middle Ages world. Gone is the movement toward the mystical understanding of God's Presence in everything as we see with St. Francis of Assisi and Bonaventure and Eckhart. He is right back where he always was, the Brutus male whose characteristics work so well in what is a redefinition of the world of might-makes-right. A world that seems to advance in its physicality through science, the advent of industrialization, commercialization and capitalism, social sophistication, individualism. We are now so smart, as we control our environment to such a considerable and growing degree, that we are ready to tackle anything. No longer are we faced with the ten-foot grizzly bear in the woods with only a spear. We now walk on the hide of the grizzly who adorns our floor. We believe that we use our dominance, our self-centeredness, our competitiveness, our hierarchical nature and organizations, etc. to the benefit of mankind. We are invincible because we have redefined what is right, how the world turns, and what you must believe in order to live with "me".

In hindsight this human male Brutus persona's brilliance has done many great things materially for mankind and even given us some non-material understanding that has benefited all of us immeasurably. But, but, it has also resulted in the taking of life both physically, psychologically, and emotionally and rests on the corpses of millions upon millions of dead bodies, all children of God, who never realized their true potential to humanity and the Cosmos. Is this not always the result of relativism?

I know best, he says, and I have rationalized away any chance that there is a God who created all this Cosmos that I now dictate and His ability through His Incarnation to be part of it all.

However, the reason it has not worked out perfectly, i.e., the Brutus, male persona, is that it is

> **"in essence not what was meant to be."**

Many would question! But as noted, this evolving human male has made and given us the world we live in which has increasingly become a better world for all, or at least most! The Brutus male persona has served us well, if but brutally at times. Man's social evolution has taken care of many longstanding social issues through various social institutions of living and governing and has brought most of us into a world that no longer requires the toil our ancestors had to go through just to survive. Science has splendidly provided us with longevity never dreamed in most of the time man has been on the earth. In addition, science has helped to allow the importance of the participation of women in society around the world. People care about one another more. We rush to help others in natural disasters. We live more in community, now a global community. This is what it was meant to be! Isn't it?

> **"in essence this was not what was meant to be."**

The world of Brutus that defines in many ways most men has served us well and to those with faith it might well be said that elements of this evolution of man has been blessed by God. We have not even as of this date blown our planet up through a nuclear war. We just need, "to keep keeping on", to use a popular expression and all will work out well. After all, now we have true rationalization, modernism, individualism relativism to the extreme resulting in the modern liberal interpretation and acceptance of almost anything. There are no more taboos as I, Brutus define them!

Yes, again, indeed this male domination has served us well but to steal a phrase from microeconomics, "the calculus or change in social marginal utility is in a downward curve whose downwardness is increasing". In short, this system that has lasted forever is no longer delivering in the way we need for it to deliver. Nor are the results of the derivatives used by rationalism, modernism, relativism, and individualism bringing us a better world. Their results are bringing confusion with shifts of who or what is an "unfortunate" and the redefinition of utility and who has and who does not have utility! Who should be allowed to live and who does nothing for the rest of us? It is all about the breakup of the movement to even greater community in the world through the triumph of individualism. No one tells me what to do or what is right or wrong. I, in the spirit of the Brutus defines that for you in my terms. Even when I help others it is for my benefit first. This is where rationalism, modernism, relativism, and individualism has always led. Never, never to greater freedom nor to community. It always leads to greater self-centeredness at the expense of others. This is the evolved result of the Reformation and the Enlightenment and male dominance, a world where man is the only thing and each man defines his own existence at the expense of everyone else. This is the only logical end of rationalism, modernism, relativism, and individualism and it will not take us where we need to go in the social evolution of our world because the end result is always, "nowhere".

"in essence (it is) not what we were meant to be."

Though women in this relativistic world now seem to be more prominent has this really changed the attitude of the Brutus persona concerning women? We would suggest that these Brutus characteristics are still born out in the male's view of and treatment of women and their attitude toward women. They usually trust and love their mothers, but when it comes to other women, they generally struggle to trust them. Why, because the male is still:

- Self-centered, egotistical and domineering

- May use his false persona to appear to care for others, be compassionate, and loving and employ it as a ruse to influence women.
- Impatient
- Jealous
- Possessive

AND HERE IS THE BIG NEVER SPOKEN TRUTH:

IN THEIR PSYCHE MEN EVEN FEAR WOMEN MORE THAN ANYTHING ELSE!

Men would rather be facing our ten-foot grizzly bear only armed with a spear than to deal with the feelings associated with a woman! Why?

BECAUSE HE NEITHER UNDERSTANDS HER NOR DOES HE WANT TO! AND FURTHER HE FEARS HER KNOWING WHO HE IS! WHY?

A man can lose in combat. He understands that. A man can lose at a game. He can handle that. A man can lose his livelihood. He can adapt. But loosing, i.e. being rejected by a woman is something he truly fears. This is true failure in life. Rejection by a woman will devastate him; possibly forever. Men may be dominant in physical male/female relationships and be the aggressor, but women have the "first right of refusal" in most of today's world and they will often use it in the cruelest, most illogical fashion. More on this when we talk about how women react to the Brutus male.

So how does he handle this? He handles it by being his Brutus male persona! That somewhat insulates him from his true feelings by seeing women as subordinate and something way less than God had in mind as a companion. It fits well into his false self.

Allied with the characteristics of the male just noted this male persona tells him he cannot really trust women. He knows he is susceptible to being manipulated by women. Therefore, women are all liars or cannot be trusted, except of course, "mom". This may not be their paramount thought, but you can bet a piece of it is somewhere in their psyche. Of course, the male would never admit this. However, women feel it and often in a big way!

They have little real respect for women because they do not understand them. The male does not care what a woman thinks. Nor, I might add, do they want to. To understand them a male has to give up some of his self-centered dominance which he thinks is wrong. God made them different and the male should not try to understand them. That's all. End of story.

Women are weak in all departments, are emotional and do not make sense. That is why they are subordinate. Therefore, I as a male, will be respectful to them externally but have disrespect for them internally.

To defend against their possible devastation of my psyche the man will hide his true feelings from the woman even if he can figure out what they are. The male will try not to have deep conversations with the woman, he will try to avoid certain subjects altogether. He will rarely even discuss sex, one of his focuses with his partner. Why should he? He is the dominant one and it's not about her in sex. It is all about him. She has to like it. And he doesn't ever know if she does or if she is just faking. Can't trust her and he does not want to know. Sex is all about him. Period.

Men want women like a moth yearns for the light but like a moth they also fear the woman because she can do him harm or even worse burn him. And like a light she is a mystery; and he feels he never really understands her. He speaks English and she speaks French and he is afraid to learn French and she does not know that she needs to teach it to him. The only time they safely get together is with sex where no words are needed and they both enjoy (hopefully) to some degree the experience.

What he really fears even today are all of the other creatures and men that could be out there in the same forest that he cannot see and therefore he cannot truly understand the situation he is in. This is not unlike his relationship with women. This is his fear of the unknown, the mystery. With a woman he can have sex with her and understand that, but he cannot understand anything else about her because she acts differently and feels differently. She remains unknown and mysterious. He thinks that since she was taken from the rib of Man (Adam) she should as the Hebrew's thought be a copy of man, but she looks different, physically and emotionally she is not a copy of the man. Again, she is mysterious to him! Men don't know they don't know her so they cannot adjust their thinking to her because they don't understand why they don't know her. They don't know what they don't know. Since men fear the mysterious, they do not try to understand how the woman thinks and acts differently emotionally and otherwise. He, therefore, does not want to get too close. He spends time at golf, hunting, etc. and away from her. Since they do not speak the same language and are not aware, of that they tie up in many ways with one another. Men are not aware they can enter the woman's world and that he can teach her how a man thinks, and acts and she can teach him how women think and act. When these conversations possibly occur, they are contentious around gender stereotypes.

The man often becomes hardened to the woman because of the sexual games she plays, often with her not even realizing that she is playing a game. She says "no". She has just rejected him, his worse fear. Then he doubts whether when she does say "yes" she is being honest. How is he to know? Even if he does not "just use her" but loves the entire woman (body, mind, heart, soul) deeply and unconditionally he may not be certain of her mind and heart's state of being.

Being extremely reluctant to expose their real selves, men spend most of their time as a male oriented false self with Brutus persona elements that may not be who they really are. They think they must be ruggedly handsome, strong, quiet, in control of their emotions and not open to others. Men have real fears that overly influence them – fears of failure, fears of not being a "man", fear of losing control and above all being rejected by a woman. They feel that if they provide, protect and give the woman children they are good partners. Nothing else is needed. However, living in the false persona takes its toll on the relationship with a woman. He is content to not open himself or his feelings to the woman for fear of not being a real man! Oddly, he thinks she will think less of him if he is willing to share his feelings with her. To overcome his fears, he must truly love her unconditionally and been converted majorly in some way to not care about the persona or the fears anymore. She is worth it and worth giving it all up for her.

The result of staying in the Brutus persona male mindset is that the man and the woman with the exception, of "suspect sex" are unable to communicate about the intimacy and relationship that is the most important part of their interfacing as lovers. Typically, this shows that they are not taught that men and women think, and handle emotion differently even communicating with different word interpretations. They move away intimately from one another by moving apart physically, spatially, and emotionally, the result of the relationship becoming sick. This leads to their relationship always being in a state of competition, and argument instead of love and discussion. Now one must win and the other lose! This is not companionship; this is not what God had in mind. This needs to stop! This is just "use."

As the Brutus he will be the dominant one in finances and all matters with the buck stopping with him. And if there is a problem, he will fix it and he will fix her and all her problems. Don't need to spend forever listening to her about it.

Also, a good way to avoid all these sticky male/female situations is for him to be what society says is a good mate. That means the three P's, PPP, Protect, Provide and Propagate. This makes the male a good mate, husband and maybe even father in his mind. That is all that is required. I don't have to get to know her or even tell her I love her all that many times. I prove that in bed. Right? I don't have to discuss intimate issues with her, I provide for her and I protect her. That shows my intimacy and love for her. I don't need to talk about it. I gave her children. That gives her something to do. I can easily admit and believe that she is kind, nurturing, compassionate and can rear kids really well. Therefore, I don't really have to do anything else. I just need to play with the kids and show them a good example of what a real man is like. And I think I know what that is like. I am not sure my dad was that way. But I will try to set a good example through sports and outings. I don't need to talk to them about values and love and stuff. She will do that.

THERE IS A PROBLEM WITH ALL THIS. AND MOST HAVE NO IDEA WHAT IT IS

BUT THIS ALL IS DIFFERENT IF..........
we will speak to the "IF" later!

LET'S CONTINUE TO LOOK AT THE EFFECTS OF DOMINANCE/SUBORDINATION.

In a world that rules by physical power and might, it determines what is right, and in turn there naturally develops a society that is hierarchical in structure and that demands longevity. Groups obtain power violently and violently try to keep it. Male physical dominance is only exaggerated by the physical issues regarding propagation that continuously affect women making them even more unable to participate, let alone survive in a "might-makes-right" culture. Thus, society in almost all cultures develops along male dominated, female subordinated lines in a hierarchy. The natural intense sexual lure of the man to the woman places the woman in a greater degree of subordination as a "use-oriented victim". When the male dominates due to physical ability and sexual desire with little cultural constraint the woman becomes even more of a product for "use".

And this male dominance affects our view of community and how community operates.

IN CONVERSATION

Sherri: *"Wow Bob that seems harsh concerning who men are and what their thought process is. Do you really think that all men are like that? I don't think I would have had such a severe list of characteristics of men."*

Bob: "Sherri, I think you have seen many if not all of these characteristics in men if you give it thought and I see them in men in all different venues. Now, this does not mean that all men have all of these characteristics, but I see them, and they get in our way of relationships, companionships and community. These characteristics are all about 'me'."

Sherri: *"Bob, I am not sure how we move from the characteristics of the human male/Brutus male to the discussion of relationships, community and companionships?"*

Bob: "Good question Sherri! And another question I have interest in, 'how do women respond to these characteristics?'"

Sherri: *"Yes, Bob and how has and does a woman, the 'companion' talked about in Genesis respond to a man with these characteristics? How do her characteristics help her move toward the end of being in relationship, into companionship with him?"*

"Let's look at the woman, 'Flesh of My Flesh' to give us insight!"

BEHOLD: THE WOMAN

"THIS IS FLESH OF MY FLESH"

Adam could see it because he had not yet fallen into sin! He knew that from his rib emerged, the, "flesh of his flesh, bone of his bone". Adam knew as did ancient Judaism that the rib bone meant everything, a complete duplicate of him, a woman, his equal, his helper, his companion, yet beautifully and wonderfully different! The perfect companion coming from the perfect God, made just for him!

But their sin got in the way of, "what God meant to be". Sin brings for each of us an alienation from what is wonderful and what is true happiness, i.e., God. What was meant, companionship, would have to wait! God was ready, we were not. So, in God's time, never in our time, God would bring them to be what was meant to be – true companionship of man and woman!

As part of God's plan, He first brought man into the world through His gift of Creation. He then established His covenant gift with the corporate group of Israel. From this heritage of the covenant relationship He through a human, Mary brought the gift of Jesus the Christ, God Incarnate, God dwelling with man. In our day He has continued His presence and His gifts to mankind through the gift of technology – God's gift to man to transfer his nature for the good and progression of spiritual evolution toward salvation.

God Incarnate would assure that man and woman would become companions for the sake of mankind! God was not cruel, missing or angry for eons of time. He simply was being who God is, complete love, waiting for his human children to evolve enough in maturity. He had shown them a nation that He blessed, He had been born a human man Himself to be Incarnate in man's world, He had given even the Incarnate One, the Crucified One, death to show his eternal love for mankind.

In our time He has allowed us to discover the gift of technology! And who do we suggest will benefit from technology? – the woman, the companion that will become the creature she was meant to be. She, his helpmate, his companion comes to do God's will as the future unfolds. But it will take the dominant one, the male, to realize the need to change into who he was meant to be by transformation while never compromising his identity as a man. He, with Brutus characteristics, has to be transformed into a "new person" and he will be the one that will end the dominance/subordination era and be the force that will bring in the new era that was meant by God in the Garden, the era of man and woman as companions. But we are not there yet in our discussion of God's gift of technology. We still must better understand women's reaction to the dominant gender.

Women living in a subordinated existence for thousands of years seem just part of the way society has been, is and should be. Even though their personal safety and society's view of them in general has greatly improved in most of the world still in the back of their minds and often well-hidden may be a basic physical fear of men. In their hidden conscious the woman knows that the man is physically superior and has done and can do her great physical harm. This is a possible subconscious fear in all women that has stayed with them into our day. They die by the hands of men daily. She knows she can be killed by a man – the refuge of an era that has begun to pass. Therefore, she may be able to love her children unconditionally. She will gladly die for them if warranted. But a man she can never love as much as her children, i.e., unconditionally for he is dominant and deep inside her she fears and mistrusts him. Why would one expect anything else? She has at least thousands of years as proof.

She often seems to have no voice in society except in her relationship with her children and she suspects that even the man she loves in most cases has little true respect for her opinion. Although she, like the male, is a social being living in community, her only voice is typically in her community of women. A voice means not only that you are heard but that you are also considered and understood. Neither has been the legacy of the woman in the world of the man.

Therefore, the woman, the modern woman, is the product of a legacy of subordination. Physically and psychologically and in most of history socially she has been tied to the man who in marriage is the head and defines both of them as one, his one, his name. She has been dependent upon him for everything and still in many societies she is nothing without him. She has feared the stigma of divorce which in earlier eras often meant poverty and death and that suggests she is no longer of value and often has no choice but to stay with him no matter what and of course the worn out but often true statement, "for the good of the children". She does not even have to love him.

She may however fear not being attached to a man. She can easily fake the rest. With children he may appear to her as simply a financial support mechanism to be played as only a woman knows how. Her social savior is a "family" because in the family she can and often is an authority, less subordinate but with a voice. You can't blame her. This has been and is her way of living through subordination. It has worked for a very long time!

But the psychological toll on her has been great. Often being subordinated in society gives one that constant undercurrent feeling of failure. Combined with her natural feminine characteristics she is often seeing herself as not quite measuring up. She is willing to take the blame for failures of all types. She must be in the wrong, or incorrect or not good enough to be in the right and have done the right thing, i.e. done what the male would have just naturally done. Therefore, she is often willing to take what she deserves by tolerating physical, verbal, and psychological abuse. She is also more than ready to sacrifice herself for others to prove her worthiness. She is society's willing victim and at least being a victim gives her another version of "voice".

She realizes that without a true voice and being subordinate she hopes to find consolation in those like her so she tries to form or join a "herd", a group of women friends that will give her the venue for a voice and the companionship she usually cannot get from a man. The herd gives her a sounding board that helps her cope with her subordination, gives her a place to vent her anxiety and a place that will often protect her from men and herself. Failure to find or create this herd leaves a woman out in the desert and very subject to a greater degree of the wiles of the male. Even if this herd is made up of her relatives, she is better off than to be alone with no friends.

Those like-her are like her in the characteristics of a woman because they are all made in the image of God with the characteristics of relationship and companionship. They have everything God wanted them to have even though the ones they were built for do not recognize it, the males. Even though they complete the male he is oblivious to it because he exists only in his own world of Brutus and general dominance.

Those female characteristics allow her to see all of life in a much broader way than is true with the male. She has had the luxury to look at things more broadly and more slowly in order to better understand her environment. There is no grizzly bear staring her in the face!

She is then able to look at all possibilities in her version of logic which takes into consideration many more of her senses than is typical in males. This allows her to bring into play "emotion", a word often feared by males. A woman being emotionally wise categorizes a key trait of the woman that is often viewed negatively by men but which in effect shows the woman for the real person she is. She isn't hiding behind a false self and its persona. Without emotion can you truly be a human being? And oddly being emotional is only bested by the male if the truth be known. He in fact is very emotional. He has just had to hide it very well. As we have noted, emotion does not work well in hunting and war!

Another characteristic of the female that has suffered greatly at the hands of men seems to be that she is seen by males as too talkative. In New England women were even fined for talking too much! But isn't it ironic that talking is a form of communication that defines us as a society and community with relationships wherein talking and communication are absolutely necessary and valued? What so easily can be misjudged is negated through talk and understanding. Please note that humans have slowly learned to talk more and fight less which is why we still exist as a species.

Women have all the characteristics that can help keep our species alive and thriving. They are loving, relationship oriented, compassionate, nurturing, kind, good, giving, not time-stamped, willing to open up their heart and mind to others, emotional and tender-hearted, sacrificial, enduring, surrendering, generous, non-violent, peaceful, more spiritual and open to spirituality, and thanks to their subordination often not in as competitive one-up-man-ship as are their male counterparts.

Many of these characteristics are also in the anima, the feminine principle of the male subconscious but he may be unaware they are there.

However, they are there, and they play out in eternity by becoming his spiritual side which may allow God to convert him into a real ordered human being and a companion. Women would seem to be more willing to have a spiritual side of their life and seem to be more drawn to God and spiritual things. This may be because she in fact is more like the companion and therefore more like what,

"God intended", more made in the image of God, more willing to be subordinated to God. He is also able to be in relationship, community and companionship but he has no idea he does and suffers from living in his false self.

In relationship to God the woman may feel she comes up short in relation to the mother of us all, Mary, but this is because the woman often views Mary, not in the context of a human woman but as some supernatural entity that she feels is so far above her that it is hard for her to relate to her on a daily basis.

But the feminine characteristics of the woman and her spirituality allows the male to have mothers and wives and female friends that challenge the Brutus persona and show him especially through our mothers the way mankind was created to be, "what God had in mind".

The subordinated has the characteristics that should have made them dominant or at least companions!

Brutus may have trouble relating to Mary in the same way that women can relate to Jesus. There may be some natural attraction in the relationship between women and the Incarnate God as a man, Jesus. The woman may be able to relate to the man Jesus by being able to relate by loving and surrendering to the physical male Jesus in the way that she surrenders to a human male.

Jesus, as we will suggest is the true man not seen before or since.

God then comes to the male through the woman who is more like God in her characteristics than the male in her role of companionship. Man cannot be as close to God as the woman because she is more like God than the male and is able to surrender, love, etc. to the man Jesus. The woman has a more intimate relationship with God because of her capability to love with all of her senses and surrender by showing the love in her ability to love her children almost unconditionally.

The male can only enjoy this type of intimate relationship with God through the woman which is what God intended or through direct divine grace to the male by God. Therefore, most males can only come back to God in an intimate love relationship via or through the woman. Sadly, most women have no idea that this can occur.

The woman as a conduit to God for the male makes her far more important than just a release of sexual tension. The complexity of the relationship between men and women seems even more complex than we live it day to day. Psychologically, between the two sexes, there are many complexities that hinder the woman being the needed spiritual conduit for the male. We know the mystery is there but since it flows beyond just the physical and the social, we seem to lack understanding as to the importance of the whole relationship.

Writers such as Robert Spencer and other depth psychologists suggest that we can understand relationships through understanding myths and the characters in the myths. In explaining the male urge for the woman that is other than just animal physical instinct we might as Spencer puts it, see projected psychic images as "invisible partners" in relationships that are greatly affected. The person carrying the projected image is either greatly overvalued or greatly undervalued by the other, i.e., the person carrying the projected image will greatly attract or repel us. We also see this in Ignatian Spirituality as we explore our true selves and/or false selves.

At first the woman is flattered and valued by the attention she is receiving from the male because of her projected image upon him and she may even enjoy a feeling of considerable feminine power. But the man will often begin to suffocate her and not be happy that she is not always available to him and thus an oppressive quality is added to the relationship by the male in his attempt to control her. He is seeing her not as she really is but as he wants her to be. His dominance seeps in and begins to take over. When she insists on being herself the man may be jealous, resentful and pouting. His attraction may be more sexually urging than is his interest in her as a person. The male may not understand her need to work out their human relationship first before or at least along with the physical contact.

In God's economy of salvation, He made the woman equal to her mate but "different" as we noted. That difference is key to their potential for "companionship". Women by nature have unique individual characteristics which we have noted, but she also has key group-forming characteristics that are relationship and community oriented and that defy any version of a current society and its culture. Yet these characteristics are subject to her subordinated place in her world governed by the male of her day and his view of her.

So, in a very great sense she is always seeking relationship, community, and companionship but in continual reaction to whatever the male is of her day. But being in continual response to the male implies that she has little or at least limited real opportunity to be the initiator of anything associated with the male. In reaction to him as initiator she may act in a way that is foreign to the male.

The "difference", of her natural focus on relationships and community defines her role for herself in her community of the family. This role is softer in nature and more open to these two key human characteristics of relationship and community than the male. Her more encompassing view and understanding of her surroundings, i.e., her ability to take in all elements of an entire situation with all of her senses gives her a more broad view of her relationship with her environment and its characteristics and the other humans that make up that environment. "She sees these things broadly". She has not had to be myopic in focus in order to react swiftly and decisively in a "might-makes-right" zero/sum world. This allows the slowing down of the assimilation of all the elements of a broader view of a situation to some degree and therefore allows her a greater understanding. With greater understanding may come greater acceptance of the situation, the people involved and lead to more options, allowing a more nondualistic view of any situation.

This is not to suggest that a woman is unable to make quick decisions if necessary, but it does imply that her decisions may be better based given her broader view of time and environment. This female view can potentially provide a balance and a more thorough/complete contribution to the companionship with the man. With her relationship building skills of love, friendship, acceptance, nurturing, compassion, emotion and above all empathy she fosters the non-judgmental, non-dualistic attitudes that allow people to fail in relationships and yet not destroy the relationships. They provide for environments that help negate the win/lose, zero/sum, one upman-ship of the male world that places strife and often means short-term relationships that inhibit the development of community.

Then, given her characteristics, what is it that truly influences who she is, her sense of who she is, her purpose, her acceptable behavior, her feeling of contribution and well-being? Her relationship and community characteristics and skills give her a unique purpose in procreation and child development. Oddly though, she may view herself as unsuccessful in life in all these important community building areas unless she is successful in the way her male dominated society defines what is success.

In her subordinated yet important role in reproduction, sex is often a source of potential mental conflict for her. She yearns for the sexual attention of the male because it should lead to relationship, community and companionship. But there are aspects of it that may actually haunt her and make it a less enjoyable part of her life. She may be haunted by the first time she had sex. Was she raped or taken advantage of by a relative at an earlier age, did she succumb to peer pressure telling her do it now "the time is right"? If she had sex thinking the man would marry her or if she had pre-marital sex with her future husband, the negative effect of sex may be less with her. If not, the haunting may have to do with her having sex with multiple partners, problems in establishing new relationships with men because of her sexual history, as well as the innate fear issue of men that she carries with her in her subconscious. All of these issues may stay with her as regrets and affect her relationships whether she is young or old.

As one might expect she is greatly influenced by her society that places success in authority, money, power, etc. instead of in the community building skills she naturally possesses. She may even falsely see herself as being inadequate to serve in many capacities. Even when she does become a leader it is often reflected in her acting like, "just another male"!

Her broader view of relationships utilizing a balance of input of senses, acceptance, time, etc. combined with the situation of the moment brings her to relationships that include the heart as well as the head. This people oriented nature goes beyond just the head, and logic of the moment. Her broader view allows her to exercise relationship in a way that extends beyond the task answer of the moment and allows her to be in communion with a greater segment of community than is possible with the male. She is then able through empathy to tie into her own feminine community. In general, carrying common experiences with her feminine community such as those of common shared views and reactions concerning her physical feminine health, her general reaction to the male dominated society, and the many aspects of her relationship and community building skills helps to develop her social orientation.

For example, hypothetically, if there were no men and no legacy placed on women by male domination, women might very well organize around the characteristics of each woman in a group who were being organized to complete a task, instead of having the task being the focus. The focus would be on the feminine manifestation of the female characteristics of the individual woman in the group and that would determine the best woman for a specific sub-task within the overall prime task. The male would have focused on the task itself with less regard to the individual person assigned to a task and their characteristics with possibly less emphasis on the individual's attributes to perform the task well.

Another example that is more current would be a situation where a woman has hierarchal responsibilities for others or just men. In these situations, a more feminine approach to authority might involve the neutralizing of the gender element by refocusing an issue on the group instead of the individual involved and their contribution to the task. This helps to remove the gender element and make it a common responsibility of the group. This fosters relationship and community building within the group.

Since women are relationship and community building oriented by nature a key element is the ability to have empathy for others, i.e., to understand and appreciate others. This idea of empathy as a key component of the woman cannot be understated. This empathy seems to be a natural characteristic of a woman. When empathy is poorly developed in a woman it might imply an unhealthy emotional state or forced forms of behavior training that have compromised her natural empathy. For example, if a woman is trained to do everything a man is trained to do in a way that a man is trained, she must be careful how she exercises her authority, or she may lose the respect of the men that she leads.

This general shared empathy with other women and her culture as a whole is due to her broader view, a reaction to her status in society, and her shared empathy with other women and often children in their formative years. This shared empathy is seen as she deals with individuals on an individual basis when her frame of reference is other than the influence of the male.

Thus, from these observations we might draw a conclusion that women have the ability to view things in life differently because they are women and they are different. Therefore, to further our previous example if they were left alone in a non-male society they might well base all types of decisions on their natural relationship and community building characteristics, decisions being made based upon people-oriented criteria such as personality, emotions, etc. of the individuals with major empathy for the person and their ability to know where the person's possible failure might be oriented. From this she understands that the criteria are not the Brutus male criteria of hierarchy, authority, competition, time obsession, control, ego and task.

For the woman to exercise her relationship and community characteristics in the past and in the present the woman often has had to exist in her culture in a state of being as if in a counterculture. Therefore, a woman will understand intuitively that she is subordinate in a male dominated world and live two very different roles at the same time in response. She may very well have no idea that she is doing this. She will acquiesce to her culture even to the point of not really understanding that she is doing so by allowing the male to make the more important decisions in their relationship without realizing it. What is meant by relationship here is the woman's relationship with any man.

Since women naturally desire relationships, she may unwittingly mistake any male's attention and lust factor for a woman as a sign that he desires a relationship with her, and she will try to turn that attention into a relationship regardless of the apparent difficulties. This helps to insulate her and her children from the results of subordination – the need for protection, provision and propagation especially in the world of the "might-makes-right". If she can become something more than a sexual use option, she can possibly become more of a counselor, influencer to the male and the male culture even if this is only on a one-to-one basis. Further, the relationship she builds with the male may provide children which he values. The children become a common result of their relationship that the male may see as important for many male-oriented reasons. It also gives the male a reason to acceptably show love and affection which requires justification in the eyes of other males. This is a start for "companionship" between the two and helps to put a crack in the armor of Brutus.

IN CONVERSATION

Sherri: *"It has been difficult for women over the centuries to enter into a true companionship role with a man given her subordinated state in the might-makes-right world. She has truly had to form relationships based upon his ability to provide, protect and propagate. She, like him is not being her true self. It is hard to be an authentic person with that legacy and try to be a new person."*

Bob: "Yes, it is. Both man and woman struggle to understand the uniqueness of the other and appreciate their strengths. Being different is a blessing from God. Yet males still struggle to understand the female and her role in his life."

Sherri: *"Why does it seem men do not want to understand women and why is it difficult for him to accept that she is different from him?"*

Bob: "A man knows that a woman is different, but we don't really understand why? Sometimes women are too mysterious. We want women to be equal, but we don't want them to be men."

Sherri: *"Good point."*

BEHOLD THE WOMAN

BONE OF MY BONE

The crack in the armor of Brutus existed interiorly as we are reminded that Adam knew that the rib bone meant everything. God created woman as a complete duplicate of Adam, his equal, his helper, his companion, yet beautifully and wonderfully different! The perfect companion coming from the perfect God, made just for him! With Brutus there is little room to understand and receive care from the helpmate and companion that God gave him. She is quite different, but he doesn't have time to understand her thoughts and emotions let alone see her as more than usable chattel. Her way of thinking and living might only put the male at risk in protecting, providing and propagating.

Within most men there was little room for the God-like soft values of the woman. Truly the survival of the fittest was not far from reality for most men. The only hope for the woman in a world that did not value her qualities was to be subordinated to the male for all areas of protection, provision and propagation. She became "use" and less human, less a companion and a helper and more in the physical than the psychological sense. He had to provide for her, use her sexually and propagate children to help him in his future survival. Sometimes there may have been a derivative of love as we romantically think of it today but the difficulty of making this happen formed the limited expectation that such a thing would happen.

Because of this historical reality and their physical differences men and women made this dominate/subordinate the social norm. Only when a woman was in a unique position in society or was a key to the continuation of a group already in power or through the woman being a bargaining chip did she become something other than the norm.

Through the predominance of sin, even if socially evolved without intent because of the environment, the "helper", the "companion", became of little concern in the decisions of the man and woman. As we have said, she was thought of as an object of "use" in many ways, a chattel to be bought and sold symbolically, or actually.

For to be dominant instead of dominating could suggest a reality of goodness. To dominate the other usually involves ill intent. To be dominant over another, would imply an elevated position or ruling position but that would then imply one who was equal to the dominant one but willing to be ruled over.

Dominating was more the reality. The woman could not be understood by the man, so she was dismissed as something "less". She became the "use victim" and the product of evil and sin. She could have been the companion of the man, the other perspective, the one "like God", the one who made the psychological and physical man a True Man. But she was not. Not in the mind of the Jew, the ancient Persian, the Asian nor the Greek mind!

But there was an end to this mismatch, and it would begin soon but not come to fruition for another two thousand years.

Therefore, the Brutus male viewed the woman as something different and through her dependency on him he was not able to understand reality. This relationship between men and women, has been the general state-of-affairs until the present.

With women being functional property chiefly for propagation, the concept of romantic love between a man and a woman is a more recent development. One might argue that romantic love as betrayed by

"Hollywood" in any era is often more love of oneself than true love and does not seem to lead to long-term relationships of companionship. Women were "used" for sexual gratification by the male hidden behind the disguise of propagation and responsibility. But with this use of the woman came the protection and providing for the woman by the male. She became important property if subordinated property. She became more than just a human producer. She became important in the organization of society and in norms and laws regarding property ownership and succession of that property and its ownership. She had to be "pure", i.e., show clear ownership via the proof of her virginity before marriage. She must be "intact" so that physical property had a distinct owner and that owner was the only owner. And in "most of our history" this meant that she had little say in who the male companion was with always a major concern for her own safety and well-being for herself and her children. Her uncorrupted nature gave her the ability to determine heirship which meant that all property stayed in the family and assured there would be enough potential heirs living long enough to keep the property in the family. Any action to compromise unnaturally this ownership alliance was disruptive to society as a whole. Marriage was meant to cement this current ownership and the perpetuation of that ownership. However, this subordination led to some degree of true organization and property laws that have served us well despite their reason for being.

However, on a more emotional level marriage was and still is so ultimately important to the woman. Through marriage she experiences her first death to self because she will never again be the center of attention and through the death of herself in marriage she will experience resurrection into a sacrificial woman with purpose and able under the probable leadership of a man and be a mother to the next generations.

IN CONVERSATION

Sherri: *"So far, we have discussed the characteristics of the male, which seem harsh and we have broadly brushed over his view of woman. But he has accepted the leadership role and being a leader is not necessarily an easy nor popular task. So as is always the case some take the role far beyond what was meant to be, they abuse or neglect it without much concern for the results/consequences. Now, let's look more closely at how the woman has responded to the man. And what drives her to build a relationship, a community, a companionship with the man using her God-like characteristics given to her."*

Bob: "Man needs her. That is why God made her to be a companion of the man. She helps him temper his might-makes-right characteristics and if allowed mitigate his often overly egotistical and competitive nature."

BEHOLD: THE WOMAN

THE FEMALE RESPONSE TO BRUTUS

Women have known little else but the Brutus male from the beginning of time. That is the way it was meant to be! Man takes the lead; woman follows and obeys. That is the way it has always been, will be, and it is the will of God!

Maybe…. not anymore!

> "The harmony in which they [Adam and Eve] had found themselves, thanks to original justice, is now destroyed: the control of the soul's spiritual faculties over the body is shattered; the union of man and woman becomes subject to tensions, their relations henceforth marked by lust and domination. Harmony with creation is broken: visible creation has become alien and hostile to man. Because of man, creation is now subject to its bondage to decay. Finally, the consequence explicitly foretold for this disobedience will come true: man will return to the ground, for out of it he was taken. Death makes its entrance into human history." (CCC 400)

The woman is his companion, his helper, not his equal in strength and might, not him in head or heart. He is God's creation, his first born. But she is his companion, ordered by God to bring him back to the Garden. She also has to run the gauntlet of the world, fight the stigma of her first mother's failure and be the one most susceptible to the evil one.

But unlike the man the woman has more of those characteristics of God. She, in her ordered state of naturalness, being who she is and who she was meant to be, is God's most beautiful physical creation, exceeding the flowers and the choral and the most beautiful array of the heavens. And she is all this beauty as a gift from God to the man and to the world. In her ordered state she is loving in a way that surpasses the man, surrendering, nurturing, sacrificial, preserver of life. In essence, she has the human characteristics of a creator of humans who loves the human creature. She is of course susceptible to the evil one because she has always represented a threat to the evil one.

She is the counter to the man in his need to dominate, lust, control, destroy and kill, the qualities needed to subdue and control the environment. She, as mother and lover, is the very essence of what the man wants to be but is inhibited by his nature and tasks and the evil one from being. In his ordered state he protects life or destroys it, but he is not life, she is life and he is never complete without her. She is the companion given to him by God who makes him whole. That is why he is so immensely drawn to her with all of his body, mind, heart and soul. His might is dwarfed and defeated by her and he would gladly give his life for her. Therefore, she and the evil one will always be at odds.

Woman was created to reveal to man something of God's love and life in a human way. She was to fulfill in her ordered state of naturalness man's wishes, to quell his yearnings, and modify his behavior, to give full weight to his human existence by being human with him, coming from him and knowing him from the beginning. This is what she was meant to be; this is her natural vocation.

The problem is that the woman has never been able to reclaim what is her true vocation her role defined by God as the companion of the man in an ordered way. Her ordered state is one of a particular nature, characteristics, roles, responsibilities and purpose meant for her by God.

Her state since Eden has always been one of misunderstanding and disorder. The root cause of this is her view of the Triune God that created her. Once out of the Garden she ceased to believe all that Eve knew about God but chose to disobey. Her view of God conflicts with God's true nature as well as His intention for his beautiful work, manifesting itself in her sexual relationship to the male.

Thus, women are preoccupied with a misunderstanding of her divine occupation and her purpose since the Garden. From that perspective much of what she does negotiates, bends, compromises her nature to be accepted by the male. In a male dominated mindset, everything she does is focused on her acceptance by the male, i.e. in what is a subservient role no matter the time or place in history. Even in her rejection of male contenders for her sexual and other favors, where she is in control, she is obsessed with him, controlled and subservient to him.

All of mankind's expectations of the conduct of the woman are magnified due to these God-like qualities given to her. Even with the woman's disordered view of God and love, even when she does not know that what she is saying, doing or being is disordered, the woman is thought of as loving, kind, moral, etc. We are all horrified when she does not act accordingly. When she in the worst of her sins kills humans in any fashion, we are dumb founded as we are horrified when she betrays as did her mother Eve. We expect her to be the moral human, the good person for God has given her many of his traits, and the ability to produce life and nurture that life through love: God>>>Eve>>>Adam, the Trinitarian Communion of God, woman and man.

Therefore, ordered woman was to be the equivalent of God's love in human form for all mankind as shown in her love for the male as his companion. Woman's arrival creates human love. In the Garden their hyper-mutual magnetism for one another creates an indescribable union of oneness that edifies their differences in a physical and mystical union of body, mind and spirit not comprehensible on this side of Eden. Thus, woman brings God's love to man as "love between two humans", something the male can now grasp and understand as mirroring the unconditional love of God for him. In the divine plan God's gift transforms the man into having the ability to love the woman in an extraordinary but subsidiary form of his love for God. Man now sees love through the woman in an intimate way only possible between a human man and a human woman.

When Adam fails in his obedient love of God and "Falls", his companion Eve also "Falls" with him and fails in her vocation. Eve's seduction by the evil one, Eve's sin against Adam, is her unique part of the curse inbuilt and passed down to posterity. Her failure to save her companion from sin in the Garden creates the curse of the poor self-image that she passes down to her sisters. The curse of the poor self-image, i.e., "I am not capable of bringing God to the male and the human race," follows woman out of the Garden and into history. The evil one uses the poor self-image to help her deny that God is with her, that she is His Beloved, that she is worthy of Him and her salvation. This disordered view of God embraces her and mankind's view of her throughout history.

Therefore, her betrayal of God and Adam or should we say her failure to do God's will and save Adam from himself, means she no longer is able to bring God to Adam and mankind as history unfolds outside of the Garden. Her real purpose for existence is well buried by her, the male and the evil one. She now becomes subservient to the male in all aspects of life because he is stronger and able to physically master the natural environment and her. She is continually reminded of her betrayal in this subservience and she sees it in the pains of childbirth and in her other physical limitations.

Again, even in her disordered view of God and love she is aware enough of her difference from the male and her unique way of interacting with him to know despite appearing to be subservient that she has power over him. As her vocation, even if she is not realizing it, God has given her the tools to make her the gift of God to mankind which can be used in an ordered way or a disordered way, i.e. good or evil. God's ultimate creative beauty given to the woman combined with her sexual draw has enormous power over the male. The Bible is littered with stories of this power used with free will for good or evil.

Countering the male qualities as his companion the woman naturally brings the joy of romance and love to the male. Man is seduced into performing them. Incapable of feeling without her as the prize he is unable to help himself since there is nothing more risky, painful and joyous than the pursuit of a woman. The male wants to love and possess and there is nothing more disastrous as we have said than her rejection of the one, he truly loves.

Only through the exercise of her unique gifts and God-like qualities of love and nurturing could she insure, the survival of the species and the love bonding to the next generation that only she as woman can convey.

Even in the ordered state of new persons' relationships of women and men there is no longer a hierarchy. But in the intended companionship created by God, the man, Adam, precedes the woman, Eve, who completes the man and is needed to save him. Eve is made by God for man as his companion. God gives Adam the role of protector of the "purity" of the woman and she is given the role of the "purity of the companionship" by fostering that companionship. This does not imply a hierarchical relationship forever, but it was justified in the "might-makes-right" era of human history if not in our post era of God's revelation through technological innovation.

The woman therefore in her willingness to take on a surrendering role as exemplified in her completely surrendering to the man in sexual intercourse is able to surrender to the man in degrees as a helper and follower in the, "among equals", companionship context with no feeling of subordination. The female is penetrated by the male in the role of servitude surrender and total submission to the male. Christ is penetrated with the spear and nails in total submission to God. There is affinity between Jesus and all women due to this intimate exchange of love.

This is the whole woman the man loves completely and wholly in the physical as well as the spiritual sense. The love of the man flows into this complete woman in a way that in eternity hints of the purity of the love that flows between the Three Persons of the Trinity.

This is seen in human sexual purity as it mimics the divine love that God has for man and can only exist in the relationship of marriage, a Trinitarian Communion marriage. The man is called by God to maintain her purity by providing her with his total love in which he loves all of her, body, mind, and spirit as he completely loves and gives himself totally to her in sexual intercourse.

An interesting aspect as to why women have accepted their role or place within a male dominated society is that women do not truly realize how important their role is in helping the man draw closer to God.

If God intended for the woman to be the helpmate of the man what did God expect for the woman to do beyond procreation? Why then is she necessary except for procreation? Why did God bother giving her intelligence and her other non-motherly characteristics and abilities? The answer resides in her community building qualities and as a companion of the male, a counselor, a helper, a component missing in the male, equal, different, but with the two becoming one and completing a community. As we have stated this companionship within their community has not generally happened and is a thought that is a more recent development in human society. But community has happened and is a fundamental part of human life. Without it we may not be healthy psychologically and socially. And what human characteristics are best suited for building these communities and crafting them to be something other than competitive bands?

In the might-makes-right world the male conquers all in the exterior world. However, some would say that the female can more easily conquer the inner world. It is the feminine qualities that bring meaning into life: relatedness to other human beings, the ability to soften power with love, awareness of our inner feelings, and values, respect for our earthly environment, a delight in earth's beauty, and the introspective quest for inner wisdom. If she, the individual, does not conquer the inner world it may well be the result of the lie of her subordination. With these qualities shortchanged, she doesn't find much meaning. With our swords and lances, males build our empires, but they don't give us the sense of belonging.

This has always been true but rarely acknowledged even by the woman. The awareness of the female, and the feminine in each of us and in our culture has been overlooked to a great degree. Everything in the world that seems to matter emphasizes a masculine side of life such as wielding power, battle, defending territory, etc. The feminine side of love, i.e., feeling, relationship, introspection, the intuitive and the lyrical experience of life have all been relegated. But in most cultures, we seldom even give "her" this due. For most women she even buys the culture's view that the inner female is a camp follower, dragged in the dusty trail of the masculine power drive, choked by wear, forgotten in a deafening and eternal clash of steel. None of us are fully aware of how much he or she is dominated by the patriarchal prejudices that maintain their illusion. None of us is fully aware to how much the masculine pursuit of power, production, prestige, and "accomplishment" impoverishes us and drives the feminine values out of our lives. We are children of inner poverty.

And how is this played out in real life? The woman is still typically considered somewhat inferior because she is different. She therefore is less than to the male and her thoughts and actions have to be mitigated by the male to make sure she does not do herself or him harm. If she wants to do something unique herself or be involved in business or organizations, she will do everything the male way. Generally, the woman bows to these realities in life and does most things the male way. She does not know another way than the male way and she does not usually use her female characteristics to devise another way. She is most often complacent with this approach to life and just lives with it! This places her in a reactive mode in most of life. She is forever reacting to the male no matter the situation. She is rarely the initiator. Women may have not considered that there might be an alternative.

Therefore, confronted with Brutus she is mostly "reactive". But her reaction is not necessarily one of agreement or cooperation. Her natural suppressed physical fear of the male and the corresponding subliminal hate that comes from the fear, the effect on her, of waking up each morning in a state of subordination in most areas of life, aligned with her daily experiences of being talked at, told what to do and how to do it, constantly remind her of what is wrong with her (goaded by the media, and unrealistic standards) and how she needs to be fixed; that she is emotional, irrational, weak in body and socialization and leadership and how this leads to a feeling of inferiority and emotional strife. When she is not one of these, she is labeled. Oddly, but not so oddly, she is seen by men as always somewhat "mad (at the male)" and a slave to her weak bodily condition.

So, she must figure out how to fight a war against the dominant Brutus male world and its values. Though perceived as less intelligent she shows an incredible mix of intelligence as she fights the guerrilla war against the male daily. She may not realize it! She will seldom admit it! She hates herself for it because it goes against her innate nature of love, kindness, warmth and nurturing. She is a community builder and her guerrilla war does not feel to her like community building.

To be more specific she handles Brutus in this way noting that "her way" comes in as many different varieties as there are women.

Where she has true power, submerged, not so well hidden at times, is in two areas, sex and the domestic home. She fully knows how sex affects the male. She knows that she has the power of sexual seduction that can take many forms and she is usually fully aware of how to use this "gift". The "gift" can be used for the building of an intimate relationship between man and woman and family or it can be used as a weapon to emotionally assault the male at his most vulnerable weakness. She can manipulate her way to whatever she wants materially or to obtain her other goals. She can, through action, i.e., denying sex from the male to get back at him for his words and actions and punish him for physically forcing sex on her or infidelity whether overt or mental.

She can often use other tactics especially with a Brutus who has not bothered to understand the differences between the genders. She does this by playing at his own game, the game of control. She does this covertly by ignoring him, relegating him to a child in her association with him and demonstrating this at home and outside of the home. This relegation devalues any authority he might have as a husband, man or father.

She does this well by dividing role responsibilities in the relationship. She is the domestic authority with almost complete control, and she reacts to him in the context of this authority. He isn't allowed to actively participate in home activities such as cooking, cleaning, decorating, deciding on what is best for the children and having any say in how she, the children or he dresses. This is her domain she is the queen and he must go along and get out of her way. She also removes responsibilities in the family that she does not want and gladly pushes them on him. Finances for example, may be handled by her because he does not want to do it. It is her responsibility. She controls the finances for her security. She may even privately go so far as to squirrel away small amounts of money due to her view of his potential future infidelity. She defers certain household tasks to him, and she may defer unpleasant discipline scenarios to him to maintain a more suitable relationship with the children.

In their personal relationship she can make the Brutus look partially incompetent to the outside world even if he is a CEO of a major corporation or a Colonel in the military. All, of these covert weapons free her from any wifely responsibilities that might help the relationship to be a closer one. With this domestic control she can purposely or unwittingly, downplay him to her friends and others as not being quite the man he should be. She can easily play the victim to all others and if he does not live up to her expectations, she can make him suffer. We, society, often tend to want to side with the woman, the weaker sex.

Most Brutus males are not savvy enough to see these things happening because in their Brutus state they have not bothered to understand women and they don't give them the benefit of the doubt in being able to exercise any control at all. The Brutus feels that he in fact is in control, when in reality he is absolutely not in control. She is winning the war that he made happen and he does not even know that there is a war and that she is participating in it. It's hard to defend against what you don't know!

****

God created woman from the rib bone of man. We propose that God's plan all along was for men and women to be equal and different from one another with the beautiful gift of diversity to compliment, one another with the idea of true companionship drawing them together. The idea of companionship is a mutually shared happiness and satisfaction within the relationship.

From the view of the woman, what is it that a woman should seek in a man if she wants to be happy and be a true companion of the male and not a secret adversary? Given the God-like and relationship characteristics of the woman she wants and seeks relationships with others.

She is looking for respect as a human being and as a human being she is seeking equality in the eyes of man. Intellectually, she is equal to the male. She is different than the male but her being different is viewed by the male as being okay. She must just accept her proper place in society. He does not seek another competitor.

She desires to be accepted for her ability to see a broader view of the world. Therefore, with her broader view of things and seeing things with all of her senses she may take longer to make decisions and that is okay with the male and society in general. She is even loved regardless of her "likes" being different from the male.

She uses her relationship building skills with others and she willingly takes the risk to foster deeper companionship. For example, she nurtures them in the community among people and animals; she fosters a positive, loyal and solid friendship between herself and her male companion as well as their children. She risks her heart trying to foster a deeper companionship with the male, in an effort to assist him in overcoming his Brutus violent nature and his tendency toward infidelity. In this risk she seeks a personal relationship with God as her helper and is often the catalyst for bringing a closer relationship of her male toward God through their union as lovers.

Of major importance is the intimacy of her sexual relationship with her male as an important and equal partner who wants to share with him the ultimate human relational experience. She wants that dialogue that two intimate lovers should want concerning all areas of their sex life. She wants to be of ultimate importance in the sexual love enjoyed between the two who are in a state of the deepest form of relationship.

She does not want to be a "use item" sexually or in any other way in life. She wants to share in the relationship. She wants for the male to be willing to talk and she wants to have a voice in their discussions and about everything in their companionship.

She wants to know who he really is. She wants to know the true self, not the false self that keeps her from knowing his real self. She wants to get to the point where her pre-conceived notions about the male are no more. She sees and loves him for who he really is.

To foster their companionship:

- She wants real and truly given companionship above all.
- She was made by God to be a companion and she wants now to really be one to the man. In real companionship she can be who she really is and share that with the male.
- She can be completely honest with her companion.
- She can feel she is completely accepted as "who she is" just as God accepts each of us "as who we are".
- She can give the companionship shared generosity, trust and mirror in the companionship the companionship of two equal, but different human beings made to be ONE and function that way in the eyes of all men and their God.

THIS IS WHAT GOD HAD IN MIND FROM THE BEGINNING!

IN CONVERSATION

Sherri: *"We have focused on how women are given beautiful gifts from God to enable them to facilitate human relationships and specifically with the man in her personal relationship. Ultimately these gifts are to be utilized to cultivate society in positive ways. What we are not talking about here is how she functions in the work force. However, traditionally women have not had the opportunity to showcase their talents and intelligence in the workforce like men. These topics are for another discussion not dealt with here."*

Bob: "Well, Sherri, I think technology is a great equalizer for this inequality. Let me explain."

BEHOLD: "GOD'S GIFT OF TECHNOLOGY"

For those of us who reject modern relativism and determinism in favor of the absolutes of natural law and natural theology we see God revealing to us the foundations for our better understanding of His plan regarding male and female humanity. Technology has lessened the "might-makes-right" approach to interpersonal behavior particularly in relationships between the sexes. Communication, education, work environments, economic opportunities as well as time consuming tasks of cooking, housekeeping, transportation, child-rearing, etc. have all been overwhelmingly affected by technology in the life of the woman.

Today's popular answers of post-modernism, rationalism, individualism, and relativism that should have made the might-makes-right world irrelevant has not done so because it has not provided the answers that change the relationship between men and woman in our new world affected by technology. The result of these individualistic philosophies is the individual, not the community. I determine for myself what is right or wrong and how to live and who should live based on my own selfish interests. Just as with chiefs, judges, rulers or kings, princes or dictators, just as with totalitarian governments, oligarchies, democracies, theocracies, and utopias they fail to understand what God has in mind for the world. The answers to our future and the God-given benefits of technology reside in a return all the way back to Eden to discover what God had in mind and has been waiting to happen since the beginning of time.

We can now begin to see the equality of the different but common natures of the man and his companion. We suggest that, God is revealing to us what is not necessarily new roles but ordered roles and how to live them out. Relativism and modernism will pass away as untenable in defining and controlling anything and will commit intellectual suicide. When everything is relative nothing moves from the relative to the real; all arguments never end in a solution and nothing is accomplished. Alternatively, God's plan in natural philosophy will with great struggle become more and more apparent for the welfare of all humanity.

The Brutus legacy now struggles in a world changing so fast. This persona needed to run the world of the past did not work well nor did societal and religious attempts to control it since it was based on a male persona that fed a dominance that lacked the cooperation of community. That attitude has stayed with us through today.

Through God's gift of technology, the male is left behind in so many areas. In a world shrinking through technology the time between the thought and the actual event has become simultaneous. This should benefit the fast thinking/fix it male, but it does not. He is challenged today by not having the non-dualistic view he needs to make better split-second decisions. Nowhere is this persona challenged more than in personal relationships which highly dominate our daily lives in new and various ways.

Technological action almost precedes our ability to think through what we are about to do. This Brutus persona has been one of necessity to get through the daily life of physical requirements on the body, and psychological and mental stamina. Even in the problem solving leading to science, the arts, etc. he feels this compulsion to decide and do. As we have noted Brutus must therefore be ready for anything in a moment's notice or be subordinated to another male, i.e. he is in almost eternal competition with all others. He must one-up another man in order to keep control. Only by being in and keeping in control can Brutus be sure of his safety and self-worth. Therefore, the only way for a man to not be in this position is to institute hierarchy, a favored male characteristic, to insure himself at least some degree of one-up-man-ship over at least one other.

To keep or obtain this position of hierarchy almost always includes violence or at least the subliminal threat of potential mental or physical violence against his own or others. Within this persona the man must be willing to subordinate all non-dominating emotions that make him dominant among other men. He must maintain his dominant position of women through the Brutus mentality played out with her.

With the passage of history and in God's time this controlling relationship and the domination and subordination of humans in the "might-makes-right" world has modified some. Or, should I say, should have modified some. Has it today changed in reality?

Yes, of course it has changed! Women are able to produce children and through science more people live beyond a few years, women survive pregnancies, work in all capacities in most human civilizations, and are no longer thought of by most of society as chattel. Women, in general, in society's terms are not as subordinate.

Except, except in the image of the Brutus persona existing in much of the male psyche!

And herein lies the problem!

All these Brutus characteristics are still in the personas of too many males. And that persona's view of women is still pretty much intact to use that word again!

Men don't like to talk about this and in fact do not talk about this and avoid any deep discussion of it. Most don't even realize that they feel consciously and subconsciously the need to be and live out the Brutus persona. This defines them as a man, "period". They do not question it. It is the only way to be! It got our world this far, don't mess with it. But the Brutus characteristics are still born out in the male's view of women and their attitude toward women. They usually trust and love their mothers, but when it comes to other women, they generally do not trust that they can be their true selves. But, this view of women is

"in essence not what was meant to be."

Let's look a little more closely at the male of today and begin to see the need to transform this modern male into a "new person man" made for the future. Understanding the past is over, it is now the time to change, a time for the man to be "who he was meant to be".

As we have said the Brutus male persona is a product of evolution - physically and socially. His characteristics define him in his relationship to himself and to society, as a whole. So, what has changed in today's world? Where is the delta that should change Brutus and make him question his own reason for being and wellbeing, let alone change his view about a woman? This was, in essence, not what was meant to be. Why are things the way they are in too many instances, and why this cannot sustain itself as we evolve psychologically and socially. What will change this? What is already changing this male persona is a gift that currently is not readily seen as a "gift from God"? It is technology! In this post-modernism world of "me, me" and our extreme self-centered focus we want to control reality, so we take all the credit for our changing world and for technology.

The reality is technology is a gift to humanity from God. We moved from being an earth centric Cosmos to a Sun centric Cosmos to a Man centric Cosmos! The real Cosmos in our galaxy is centered in our sun for us. The complete centered Cosmos is the Creator of all in the Cosmos and that is the Triune God! God determines all aspects of science and controls all as man discovers and uses technology to serve mankind. God dwelling in man continues to control history and the future of the world. Not in man's brilliance alone but in man's brilliance as a result of our Creator and His being within us. Despite the lies, of many self-centered humans God and His Church has never been at logger heads with science and in historic reality has always been part of this effort. The supposed anti-science Church has and is a pro science entity that has not allowed self-centered people to deliberately destroy other humans for their own personal benefit "in the name of science and technology".

So, why would technology even as a gift from God to mankind be a positive change in the direction of God?

1) Technology has brought most of mankind into an era of leisure compared to our previous history and mankind has vastly benefited from the application of science to everyday existence. However, at the same time has it not eroded many of our legacy moral structures and laws and given us the means to truly do evil through destructive weapons that can annihilate our whole planet very easily, actual wars continuously fought, the destruction of groups of people for convenience, the murdering of babies in abortion, euthanasia, assisted suicide, destruction of basic human rights, the destruction of our resources that we are supposed stewards of for personal gain and the endless murder of those humans who do not agree with us often in the name of some god that does not exist as portrayed? We have just witnessed the results of self-centered relativism – millions of dead bodies that highlight the 20th Century.

2) But technology has brought man forward exponentially for God's purposes and we benefit by being His human children. Despite the evil backhand of technology much good has been done, is being done, and will be done through technology. For example, raising money, sharing positivity, sharing chores, alerting people to the needs of others, and during the Corona Virus Pandemic people can help people with food donations. During "stay at home" many individuals can come together through FaceTime, or other programs that allow face to face meetings through screens, so individuals are not so isolated. Our problem as

humans is how do we use the benefits of technology morally, i.e. not as we define it but as God working through us defines it?

To move forward with God as He rolls out the future we are not bystanders since we are always the ones who do His will by delivering what He planned whether we agree with it or not nor whether we are willing participants. Technology is the catalyst for this phase of society's evolution and who will benefit most, why did God give us this gift of advancing technology? Women will!

However, predominantly, we still live with a "might-makes-right" mentality and the woman is still subordinated to the man physically.

3) Men and women no longer need to compete with one another particularly within their interpersonal relationships, they need to exhibit an attitude of cooperation toward one another. The woman, not being in physical competition or dominance has allowed her the freedom of not taking on all the responsibilities of the male in society. Our role-oriented culture allows her certain privileges that makes life more worth living and our laws protect most women legally and physically in these roles of everyday life. She does not have to put on the Brutus male persona in order to perform most of her standard roles. Yet now she is afforded the opportunity to apply for many of the roles formerly the complete domain of the male. More and more she is folded into society with less roles being denied her. The problem is not her ability to perform these roles as well as the man if not better, the problem is despite this outward appearance of equality in society the reality is that she is not seen as being an equal human being. Equality may give her a job, but it does not necessarily give her respect and allow her to be something other than subordinate. And even though might-makes-right and male dominance may be truly irrelevant in today's world it still rules the day in society less obviously but still covertly. The equality and irrelevance of the Brutus male persona still sees the woman as inferior, subordinate and not sufficiently trustworthy.

4) The Brutus male personality does not fit well with the woman as a "companion" instead of a subordinate. A companion makes her equal as a human, with the ability to be a true help mate of the man, a true equal. But to most males either fully or partially she is and always will be a subordinate and it does not matter what her title. To the male he is still responsible for the providing and protection of the woman and the propagation of the species. The idea of her being a companion seems remote to him. She is, still too different, she does not think or act like him in so many ways, she is emotional and illogical, she has health issues and at times she does not seem to be in, "control of her faculties" as once expressed. How could I trust her as a true, real and equal companion in the true companion sense?

Yet, despite his fear of her in this companion role he wants her physically, he desires her from the depths of his "being" and he wants her as a special someone to be with him. He is not sure where she fits if not as a subordinate. His Brutus male persona characteristics support his view of women. They usually love and trust their mothers, but when it comes to other women, they generally do not completely trust them. Why? Because they do not trust themselves to not use them and to act other than the Brutus male persona.

God's gift of technology is one path that opens our minds, hearts and souls to be the person that God created us to be. We, men and women are created to be companions, to be friends, to be lovers, to be the person, the new person, the human person that God desired us to be, who He desired Adam and Eve to be before their disobedience. The might-makes-right approach to life and interpersonal relationships is lessened. As men and women become new persons their desire becomes to view one another within the 20/80 perspective, as equals, as companions, as friends and as lovers.

IN CONVERSATION

Sherri: *"Well, we have certainly looked at the legacy of relationships, community and companionship and how the two sides, man and woman, have struggled to marry their two innate characteristics into forming what God meant us to be as 'companions'." Even if technology helps to facilitate a more equal balance, how do we become new persons in our world and who is an ultimate model?"*

Bob: "Yes, we seem to have one another in our lives but we are still in some confusion about how we do that. God's intent of companionship seems to still be out there in terms of what goes on in relationships between men and women. However, Sherri, with God's help we are destined to evolve into what God meant for us to be. Let's see how that might happen."

BEHOLD: THE NEW PERSON MAN

JESUS, "THE REAL MAN"

Does anyone question that the human Jesus is the personification of what God had in mind for the ultimate human male? If Jesus is 100% God/100% man, then his humanity must be truly what God had in mind for Jesus and all human males.

Jesus is the ultimate "me" – the ultimate male. Jesus is the pinnacle of the male hierarchy not unlike Mary is the pinnacle of womanhood. As males we feel comfortable with Jesus, as the pinnacle of our gender, the One we want to serve, the One we want to imitate, the One we want to obey; it is natural for males to follow a leader in the hierarchy and our ultimate leader is Jesus. Our natural inclination through our relationship with the Trinity is to go to the man, Jesus. It may be easier to go to Jesus the man than to approach God, the Father or the Holy Spirit. We must have a Commander!

Being incarnated in an earthly historical era that included a "might-makes-right" culture and male dominance, Jesus, the Christ, and subsequently Christianity brought to the world the key elements that began to move the world back toward what was meant for it to be as seen in the Garden. These elements could be seen in Jesus himself, His transformed disciples and the apostles and the empowered early Christian leaders to "turn the world around" in a direction totally different to what had ever been or known in the world at that time.

It took God himself incarnated as the Second Person of the Holy Trinity and the influence of the Holy Spirit to allow the spoken and written word to accelerate among men the truth of the Cosmos: The Holy Trinity is the creator and maintainer of our Cosmos and everything in it. We see God's redemption of mankind coming in the form of a human man, fully God, fully man, sacrificing his human life to be the savior of the entire Cosmos.

The characteristics of Jesus are also the characteristics of the new person man. Jesus shows us the hierarchy, and the priorities of life that are lived by the new person. We will contrast these with those of Brutus and show how Brutus must change to become the new person man, the ones that will establish a new era of Christianity in the world.

Since all in our Cosmos begins and ends with the Holy Trinity the model for the new person is naturally Jesus, the Christ, God among us, fully God and fully man, who brings to us, His children, the truth about all things.

Jesus did His Father's will, looking to Him to provide and then flow to others His will. Therefore, we too are to look to Jesus to understand the Father's will for our lives and who we should be as new persons guided by His advocate, the Holy Spirit.

As new persons we model Christ in the understanding that God is the Creator and continual maintainer of the universe and therefore He is continually involved in our lives and is with us each and every moment of the day. We are once again reminded of the Psalms, that we can never hide from God! He is pure love and He will never forsake us. No matter what we do He is there to forgive us for in His Incarnate form He died and took away the retribution of our sins. Therefore, He is in control and we are not! We realize that we must allow Him to control us, He is the Creator. We are not!

We believe this in all of our being, i.e., in our gut! It may be difficult for us to realize that God could love us unconditionally but through meditation and prayer we will arrive there. Once this is understood then we begin to better understand that we can have a true friendly relationship with all persons of the Trinity. What He asks of us as new persons, is to accept Him as the top of our hierarchy and our priorities in life – nothing else! Is this not the Christ talking with the Father through prayer in the New Testament?

In return we are asked to love the Trinity and try to do God's will as Jesus did, which is His will for us and all those other humans that make up the community of Christ, as well as exercise our responsibility to keep the environment He has given us to maintain. He expects us to try our best in each and every opportunity He gives us, with not ourselves as the only focus but with others also as the focus.

To accomplish, this we must not see ourselves as the center of the universe, as the one who controls. We are not being new persons when we allow the root of all evil, self-centeredness and pride, to run our lives and give us our priorities. We are asked by God to not only love Him with our hearts, souls, and minds but to always love our neighbor as ourselves. We are to trust the Christ that the Trinity will help us if we ask and in terms of all eternity be with us to preserve us. Is this not what Jesus did as He did the Father's will?

John 14:15 – "If you love me, you will keep[a] my commandments. 16 And I will ask the Father, and he will give you another Advocate,[b] to be with you forever. 17 This is the Spirit of truth, whom the world cannot receive, because it neither sees him nor knows him. You know him, because he abides with you, and he will be in[c] you."

As new persons all men and women must make the female characteristics of relationship and community building our priority in life. Our own self-worth is important and so is a healthy ego, but our focus should be approximately 20% on our self and 80% on our neighbors ("20/80 Rule"). This is doing God's will. Amazingly, it brings joy to us! By contrast a Brutus might focus on himself eighty percent of the time.

Thus, with this background of understanding the new person is and must be intentional in exercising the 20/80 Rule. As we discussed in our first book *(A Journey of a New Person, Harden Not Your Heart)* this transformation into being a new person requires one to respond to Jesus, the Christ by re-balancing their life into living as a new person in relationship to God and to others.

By intentionally saying "yes" to being the new person we begin the evolution of change in our lives into the process of bringing our mind, heart, body, and soul into "living in the Mind of Christ", to be new in Jesus Christ, to become a partner with the Holy Trinity. This allows us to be transformed in the renewal of the mind which is necessary to be new. This rebalance into the Mind of Christ means we are asked to be His Disciples, i.e. to mimic him in all of our relationships. Brutus may struggle to mimic Jesus Christ since Jesus loves and respects all.

We are willing to sacrifice our self-centeredness to desire Him and pursue Him as a way of life no matter what our venue. This may often create conflict between our false and true selves but through courage we find that our true self cannot hide from God anyway. In a sense this is a pursuit of perfection but as we have stated we can never be perfectly in the Mind of Christ, but we can intentionally try to do as Christ taught us. This then becomes our mission in life,

> **to be a true Disciple of Christ and to try to live in the Mind of Christ no matter who we are or where we are in life or in the world.**

Whereas Brutus may have his own mind and do as he sees fit, making decisions that may be to his benefit only.

Let us quickly make it clear to all of our readers that this is not implying or applying a set of laws or ascetic disciplines old or new. We have many examples of this in our Christian heritage that have given us both pain and gain. We are talking about a radical transformation of the application of love over discipline, of changing stony hearts into fleshy hearts, of nondualistic analysis of life's situations, of mercy. In short, of living in the Mind of Christ! No Pollyanna here! Our feet are firmly on the ground and we understand all too well that just as in Jesus's day there is evil in the world! But.........there is also the Christ!

As the economy of salvation has graced us in this life, to submit to God, with the Holy Spirit, and have Mary as our model allows us to deal with ourselves and others as "A Child of God" without reservation, to love our neighbor as Christ loves us! Brutus may struggle to love his neighbor.

Thus, as the new person we are intentional toward our faith by being ready and willing to make decisions each and every day and the recompense for us is what comes from living in the Mind of Christ. We experience freedom and true joy. We find counterintuitively that not catering to our false self and being self-centered allows our whole being to be able to react to the control of God who is incapable of bringing us anything other than love. We live "loving honesty". We find it easier to be social, to live in relationship to ourselves and others and we are better community builders. We look for the opportunity to bring welfare to all areas of the other, to devote oneself to others. The old adage, "it is better to give than to receive", becomes our focus in life instead of just an old adage.

The freedom comes from living a life that is transparent to God. We obey Him through our love of Christ and others, not law, or should we suggest we love Him by what the law implies, and we apply this intentionally to our others. There are no score cards. We live our way to discipleship. We try. We do not earn it. Christianity is faith, love, mercy, hope and joy!

We are now action driven in our intentionality! We change what we need to change to be in the Mind of Christ. This we can never sidestep, and none are here because this is just an evolutionary process. In many instances we need to stop one behavior and start another behavior. But we are active! We are never again complacent. Christ made it very clear that lukewarm is doing nothing! We must be committed to our change when necessary and we have to have a plan that allows this into our relationships. We must be adaptable to those who are the same or different and be able to respond to them as Jesus would. This intentional relationship building helps us to remove assumptions, comparisons and judgments concerning others from our Christian vocabulary. Brutus may build relationships based upon assumptions, comparisons and judgments because he focuses on himself and that might lead him to false conclusions about others.

Now let's consider the theme of our book and see how Jesus interacts with women.

Let's begin with **Jesus and the Woman at the Well** (The Samaritan Woman, John 4:4-42).

We see in the woman a true subordinated woman of the day. We also see Jesus as the Savior of all mankind, even a Samaritan. She is at the well at a time of day without assistance telling us she is ostracized by her own society and forced from her community. She now encounters a man at the well, but the person is not just a man who should not be there at that time of day and He is the One who knows everything about her. He asks her to help Him and accepts her by engaging in a dialogue with her. She learns quickly that this man is not like anyone she has ever encountered or ever will encounter. She has encountered the epitome of man as well as God Himself Incarnate. She immediately is aware of His uniqueness and readily sees with her broad view that He is not the typical dominating man. He brings her respect, acceptance, understanding, and hope of reentering her community. She is immediately transformed and becomes an evangelist to her own community. Her fear of being ostracized is gone. With all of her feminine characteristics she is now proud of who she has become, and she has a purpose and focus that goes far beyond herself.

In the story of Jesus and the **Woman caught in Adultery** (John 8:1-11)

We see a Jewish woman accused of breaking Jewish Law. Here we see Jesus as we are reminded; He did not come to change the Law but to fulfill the Law, i.e. to help us to understand the true nature of the Law which is Love.

We are told the woman is caught in the act of breaking the law regardless of how this was perpetrated upon her or with her. We are also reminded of a theme throughout the Gospels of Jesus as non-dualistic and therefore focused on Love versus the letter of the Law. Jesus in this story forces us as well as those who are ready to stone the woman to reflect on how much they know about the circumstances of this story.

He guides all to reflect upon their own hearts and motivations as well as reflect on what they do not know about her and the men standing next to Him. Was she a widow? Was she poor? Was she without a family male member to protect her? Was she forced into prostitution? Was she setup in these circumstances to be brought to Jesus' attention? Regardless of the details this woman who lacked status and was a use item meets Jesus as the perfect example of a new person and is therefore transformed.

Now let's see how Jesus interacts with the whole (transformed) woman in the story of **Martha and Mary** (Luke 10:38-42).

With this story of Mary and Martha we begin to understand the new person woman. As women with their broader understanding of everything through their God given characteristics, they have already perceived that Jesus is God Incarnate and living amongst them. So, we see the God given characteristics exemplified in these two women even to the point of these two women being seen together as the icon of the new person woman. So, we see the innate characteristics of the woman sacrificing for the good of all in her Martha's role and we see the heart nature of the spiritual woman in Mary. Therefore, we see the combination of these two women who together represent the new person woman.

We hope that this chapter reflects how Jesus would respond to those around Him.

- He is focused on how we love God, ourselves and others.
- He finds problems with those who find faith only in dualistic rules that no one could follow.
- He focuses on how we love one another with an awareness of evil in our midst.
- He desires us to be His disciples as new persons, male and female.
- He asks us to work on transforming ourselves in the love of Christ that passes all understanding.
- He desires for us to live in the Mind of Christ by becoming more and more like Him!

The Brutus persona may find it difficult to follow Christ freely since juggling between his own interests and those of Jesus Christ seem to be a juxtaposition.

Therefore, the new person in Christ is summarized as follows:

- God is the Creator of the Cosmos.
- God is the Trinity: Father, Son and Holy Spirit.
- The Son is Creator, Jesus is 100% God/100% Male, and Jesus, Jesus the Christ.
- God is in control of all.

- God is pure love.
- Man was made good in God's image.
- God loves me unconditionally just as I am.
- God is present everywhere, at all times.
- God has given us free will to reject or accept Him.
- God forgives when we fail to do His Will. We show our proper love for Him when we ask for forgiveness.
- God dwells in every person as the Holy Spirit.
- We believe that there is an evil one who tries to separate us from God.
- We desire to love God. We love God.
- We cannot be perfect, but we can always try to do better while striving to be whole.
- We love, praise and honor God in everything we do.
- We listen to and talk with God.
- We desire to do God's will. And we strive to do God's Will.
- We love our fellow man as Christ loves us.
- We live in the mind of Christ in everything we do.
- We forgive others seventy times seven.
- We strive never to make fast assumptions about others, make comparisons or judge others.
- We owe all to God and pray without ceasing.
- We believe The Eucharist is the ultimate earthly uniting with man and God.
- We are Christ on earth. We are the body of Christ, the Catholic Church including those Christians not in communion with Rome.
- We honor those seeking God. We honor all people as God does.
- We will be resurrected.

**This is the Foundation of being a New Person
that is who we are as a New Person**

"I am going to look at you until I see the Christ in you" - *Alana Levandoski*

BEHOLD: THE "NEW PERSON MALE"

THE MALE PERSONA LEGACY

With Jesus as the ultimate role model we begin to look honestly at ourselves with compassion and notice we view the world around us with a different set of eyes. We have a desire to change and as we change, we begin to realize a new perspective. Gone is the old Christian male's "false self" view of religion and spirituality that flows from his dominant male persona with any validity for one so self-absorbed. Gone is the old view that God typically will be a God of atonement, i.e., God as judge, not also the God of love. This is a dualistic approach to God: and it tells one what is right and wrong. According to this view everything is clear, it does not need emotion or analysis.

Then, of course the focus is sin, not love. You check off the list and you and God are "in good with one another". The Trinity is a bit of an enigma to this male with the emphasis of one of the Three Persons being more easily self-interpreted and understood. This allows the false self male to handle God in a hierarchical scheme which is much better for him to understand than the mushy concept of a Trinity with God actually inside him versus up in heaven on a throne. This also allows him to selectively take the words of Jesus to prove the rightness of his dominant male spirituality.

The Ten Commandments become dualistic, "you did, or you didn't", - "don'ts"! They are not warnings to us by a loving God but a list of actions to be "punished". And of course, to go along with our male domination the Bible is reputed to teach us that a woman caused sin!

Look at Eve, and look at treason, infidelity and adultery – all caused by a woman in the minds of the false self male. He can never move beyond his domination even when the woman is given to him as a companion. He can ignore her expressed actions of love, even when she is expressing God's love to him. Thus, he does not recognize Christ's love through her.

As society is changing Brutus may be challenged in a way that moves him beyond his own obsession.

He may begin to see "her" for her intrinsic value. He is torn between her just being a victim of his use and is haunted by her maybe being someone to honor and serve instead! When love is haunting him, he is challenged to be concerned with her needs and her well-being on a daily basis, not fixed on his own wants and whims. She is now important, and he is not sure why he has allowed himself what he perceives as weakness. This is love, no longer transitory romance, no longer the focus of ourselves on our role in the relationship. We are now true participants; we are inching toward companionship!

If embedded in his haunting is a feeling of friendship toward the woman instead of use, then will he now treat the woman in his life more as a friend than as a use item? Unfortunately, sometimes the best of us will treat those closest to us worse than we treat our friends. This often comes from not loving ourself in the right way and therefore having trouble letting the other person be who they really are. We expect them to be us and they are not. This is very hard to understand when, like the Brutus, we are unable to move beyond our nose. Friendship requires commitment and it is easier to love a friend versus a "romantic" lover because they are willing to receive love as well as to give love. Our lover must also be our friend.

The male of the early 21st Century, is caught between two worlds neither of which would be his choosing. On the one hand he is the product of the evolution of his own gender and environment in how he projects himself to his world. On the other hand, it is clear to so many that in our world and in the world moving forward the current characteristics of his persona do not fit well in the realities of today and what seems to be the sliding of humanity into the future.

He is molded for a "might-makes-right" world, but this world is fading and existing less as reality.

Brutus worked well in a primitive survival mode environment for thousands of centuries.

But what works for the male today?

AND THIS WILL CHANGE EVEYTHING! IT IS THE TIME FOR COMPANIONSHIP BETWEEN MEN AND WOMEN

To recognize who he really is?

The solution is really inside himself – who he really is versus his exterior false self.

Let's take a look into the inner life......

The true driving force today and in the future will be the end of the dominant, and the now unnecessary Brutus male persona!

The Brutus false self reigns in our world and the male domination engrained in our culture provides a perfect storm for a false self that has sustained us in a "might-makes-right" world but no longer provides us with the right tools for a spiritually oriented world. The false self is very self-centered with all aspects of life including relationships with women funneled through the self-centered filter. Therefore, everything must be clear and being clear is being self-centered but necessary to maintain pride. He must win whenever possible and show perseverance to the extreme.

We see this in so many being so focused on career or other interests that they become addicts of work, sports, alcohol, sex and whatever else they feel gives them the competitive advantage over others. This is all an attempt to obtain happiness and self-satisfaction. He is often not well rounded due to this extreme focus. Above all he is afraid to "ask" or to seek help, particularly in his personal life and he cannot allow feelings to get in the way. Thus, the model of the modern false self male is one who looks masculine and physically powerful, who seeks perfection, maintains the "Marlborough image", makes quick decisions and wins always.

This male persona is oppressive. In reality, the persona lacks dignity, confidence and real power – the opposite characteristics that the Brutus is meant to possess. He seeks happiness masked in trying to find it in business, career, or external options of life, thinking he is in community when only his mask is in community, his true self is not.

As Robert Johnson points out in his, "He, Understanding Masculine Psychology" this Marlborough image male feels the lostness and alienation of the hero. Males often exhibit a sense of injury and incompleteness. The world is not just happiness but the disintegration of childlike beauty, faith and optimism. He seeks an unconscious solution outside of himself – work or marriage, and/or place in the world. He is moody. The pursuit of these things does not seem to do it for him!

However, his psychological nature may impact his ability for any real relationships. He blames this incompleteness and unhappiness on work or spouse because he does not want to take any responsibility for it himself. He feels he has that covered as a result of being a male, living in a Brutus male's persona. He realizes that his own capacity for love, beauty or happiness is limited but he does not understand the cause of why these are limited for him. This internal paradox may make him prone to escape into pornography, alcohol, or drugs.

Living in the Brutus persona mask in most men leads to him being subject to the moods just mentioned. He is quick to blame women of being moody but certainly most men understand that they often feel moody. Be it depression or inflation moods they overwhelm him by being something other than <u>his</u> true self.

Man is no longer a master of his own house. Man engineers reality versus living it. He is afraid of real life. He does not work much on his inner life.

He does not know the inside of himself and he does not seek knowledge of himself. His moodiness is seldom admitted. Enslavement of the male persona exhibits itself through his moodiness, but he does not realize it.

Brutus men are addicted to their ways of thinking, feeling and acting and it entraps them as a drug does and gives the illusion of control and power. They are superior, they understand all that is important, and they are dualistic when the only thing that counts can be quantified and measured and therefore it is possible to be totally logical, rational, objective and right.

This mask of Brutus masculinity may be exhibited by all the Brutus male types. To convince others, particularly women, the Brutus male may often create a false persona of caring for others in order to look good, compassionate and loving when the reason for the persona is the self-oriented use of the persona as well as others. This "good look" behavior is often employed as a ruse to help get elected or promoted and very often for the sake of influencing women or a particular woman for romantic or non-romantic reasons. It does not take the Brutus male long in life to understand that women succumb very easily to this false persona because they want to believe that the man really does care about them and they key off of what they see other women doing.

The Brutus male then in so many aspects of his life becomes the loner we have been suggesting. His persona is truly his false self and he lives, a house divided, every hour of his life. He has to "act" out a role and a part that is not really who he is. He must convince others that he is who in reality he is not. And more important he has to convince himself that he is who he portrays. This creates strife he is not even aware of. This is only made worse as he lives in male dominated institutions that promote and honor the Brutus persona. He never feels whole, he never really enjoys life and substitutes activities and relationships that are not healthy to his psyche in an effort to seek happiness.

He often feels he is defeated but not sure why. His male domination seeks affirmation on an individual level, but he is up against other males who may be better in his eyes than himself. He can be a success or failure depending on how he compares himself with others. As a Brutus male he may seek validation by belonging to a male group such as an athletic team where he is allowed to individually fail and thus his failure can be taken as a community act and his actions be representative of the community and therefore less threatening to him as an individual.

Depth psychology would tell us that he is even more not in control of who he really is through the influence of his subconscious. And, of course most men have no idea of what the subconscious is or even that such a thing exists. This is even more difficult for the persona Brutus because he is not aware of the subconscious. He cannot be aware of it the way he is aware of his conscious mind. This does not mean that it is any less real. The subconscious sees images and images are harder to explain no matter how many words we might use. The subconscious also explains thoughts, feelings, and behaviors that we cannot readily explain such as a man's moodiness, a woman's fierce aggressiveness, a man's seemingly inability to make a decision when he and his gender are known for quick thinking and solutions. Even though it greatly influences male behavior how can something he does not know affect him? He sees the symptoms in his actions which helps lead him to the potential reality of the influence of the subconscious. If he is moody what might be causing that state? Could it be something going on in his subconscious?

Even though Genesis might suggest that man and woman were both one at a point in eternity we have dismissed the idea as men and particularly as Brutus males that we have a feminine side as well as a masculine side. This sounds like an attack on the maleness of the Brutus male persona! But an accepted premise of modern psychology assures us that the subconscious is real and accepted by most personality theorists and that it does have a profound effect on all humans.

For males this means we have a feminine side of our subconscious called by psychology, the anima. The anima affects the male by giving him feminine thought and feeling characteristics that are more feminine in nature such as softness, compassion, nurturing, etc. And it affects the male whether he likes it or not since he has absolutely no control over his subconscious and how it affects him. The best he can do is to suppress it if it doesn't fit into his Brutus persona or understand where these feminine natural characteristics affect him and be aware of their possible origin. If he was just aware that his moodiness might come from his anima it would tell him that he was still sane and therefore would ward off incorrect assumptions regarding his strange behavior. Of course, psychology tells us that the anima is the fountain of life in the heart of the man. She is the very core of inspiration and meaning. This gives him heart and inspiration.

Of course, the female too has a male subconscious element that will influence her to think and act in a more male way. So, when the anima in the Brutus subconscious affects the male it adds another layer of affect and influence on the false self Brutus who is already playing a role that is not him!

No one should conclude from the above that we are talking about all males being a complete set of Brutus male persona characteristics although there are many who have all of these consciously or hidden in their psyches. There are some areas of the world where almost all of these reside in most of the male population.

We would venture to say that many males have many of these personal characteristics and we can say in general that if a male possesses even some of these characteristics, they configure in him his false self and do battle with who he really is. Doing battle with oneself is stressful and may even cause problems for the Brutus in his relationships with other males often putting him in conflicts that are not warranted. In addition, when females are added to the mix it may increase the stress on the man. He may not even recognize that he has these characteristics but when circumstances present themselves, he falls into the Brutus persona.

However, with God there is always hope. As a man or woman or simply any person who seeks God there is a transformation regardless of how subtle or obvious. As a person begins to see and understand who they are and who they desire to become that is the moment or moments when one begins to understand who God intended them to be. A person seeking God's own heart.

AND THIS WILL CHANGE EVEYTHING!

**This opens the person's heart to
see others as God sees them and**

IT IS THE TIME FOR COMPANIONSHIP

BETWEEN MEN AND WOMEN

BEHOLD: THE "NEW PERSON MAN"

WHO IS THIS NEW PERSON MAN (WHAT GOD HAD IN MIND?)

He is a man of God. A man seeking God. A man whose life evolves around God and imitating Jesus's actions. Often times a man needs a catalyst to overcome the Brutus characteristic and that catalyst can be a woman or a tragic event or a life changing event. This catalyst helps him to find his true self, who he really is, who God really made him to be, and what gives him true happiness and a feeling of well-being in the world, his communities, his family, and in his relationship with God and the Cosmos he inhabits. And, when he finds this true harmony in his relationship with God, he finds his purpose and reason for existence.

A common catalyst can never be defined. At best guess it comes from some type of trauma, profound insight, awakening of the inner self, that affects him. The assumption would be that trauma would occur at a point in time but that is not at all the necessary case. The catalyst may well occur over a long period of time as he slowly comes to an understanding through life's lessons. Sometimes the believer sees in himself and in other men a slow progression or an immediate event that seems to be beyond the person and we might well suggest that this might be the hand of the Holy Spirit in his life and not just his own doing or the doing of those around him.

Certainly, an acute life event such as the death of a spouse, a child, a family member, an injury in war or the horrors of war itself or other civil or personal physical or mental strife, an illness in him or one close to him. A failure in marriage or in business or career or school, a failure of a child, prison, poverty, etc. can give Brutus the catalyst for re-thinking life and making a change.

But certainly too, this catalyst may come from "just living life", or from the influence of new ideas either personally encountered or learned through another. Jesus saw love as a transformation of the self and society instead of religion as merely a belonging system. When a man moves from the self-centered persona male to the new person man, he changes society in his own corner of the world. In addition, for our purposes this means that the Brutus persona male changing to the new person man may be more important to the woman than any legislation.

Alternatively, men in the *second part* of life may move from many of the Brutus characteristics to fewer of the Brutus characteristics and to more of the new person man characteristics. Second half of life men may have a renewed respect for the world of the heart, and a relationship of the soul based upon failure or increased understanding and the search for meaning in life through having endured life's lessons. These changes may point in a direction of new development in their lives.

Or maybe, through *awareness* that he, Brutus, is no longer the center of the Cosmos, no longer does all of his characteristics work for him, no longer does he believe he is able to control all aspects of his life, no longer can he not care about her or others in the same way he has previously. Maybe, he is tired of wining or loosing at everything. Maybe he has truly lost at something, and yet survives not thinking that a loss like this could ever feel quite so good! Maybe, having those Brutus characteristics has alienated someone whose loss is truly painful and is not recoverable.

Maybe, as a *result of an encounter with the Holy Spirit* not even acknowledged by him, he has begun to question his Brutus characteristics. Maybe it was a retreat, maybe he went to church for a change and found something other than the pride of just being there. Maybe He through the Holy Spirit has been inching into his life through his family, or work, or whatever. It makes no difference.

There may be many, many "maybes". *One size does not fit all and there is no formula.* It can be anything. But there is a catalyst for sure. And whether we seek Him in it, blame Him for it, or rebuff the idea of Him and God's intervention in our lives He may well be there through the Holy Spirit.

The result is that the characteristics of Brutus no longer work for the man and for some reason he has come to believe that maybe there is another way, something else, something that he is missing in his life. But it may be hard to believe and be fearful since the traditional characteristics define a man in our society and he fears that if he takes a different route he will fail in life.

He, through grace, is now inching toward the key to life! Maybe, I can be different. I can do things opposite of the Brutus male persona and be okay and not lose anything that is important. What's more maybe I can now be moving toward being my real self and stop being a false self that does nothing but give me inner turmoil. And he does not yet realize it, but he can now love and be loved, and he can be a companion and have a companion!

For a Brutus male to evolve into the new person he must look at life differently, become that new life and live that new life! He is now different but still ok and now a better child of God, husband/boyfriend and companion. He begins to ask daily, "why do I as a man do what I am doing?" Is he driven by his male persona who determines his day or is he driven by his God and his relationships?

Again, who is the New Person Man?

He believes in the foundation of belief that underlies the essence of the new person which explains why he exists to begin with. Therefore, he believes that the Trinity exists, that God is our Creator, that God loves us unconditionally, that God is all love, that we can be a friend of God and love Him back. He believes that God is in control and we are not; that God will take care of us throughout eternity if we stop trying to be in control ourselves. He believes that he can learn about who God is and how He works through the Word, the Bible, and through the Traditions of the Church. He believes that he does not have to suppress his emotions and feelings and he believes he can share his inner-most feelings with friends and especially women friends and not worry about what others think about him. He can begin to trust others and believe that women may no longer use his emotions against him. He believes that he can have compassion for others and show that compassion actively with those who he is compassionate about. He realizes that he does not have to win at everything or even be one-up on other males and still be a man and still be just fine. If he loses at something, he loses. He simply must try his best. This in no way defines him as less of a person or man. He can be an "active" but can also be a "contemplative" and now see a broader picture of whatever is going on and make potentially better decisions. He, too, can react to others with God, using all his God-given senses to better understand what is going on. As Paul says, "when we are weak, we are strong." Who doubts that Paul was a real man and a strong real man?

The new person man can care for others! He can have a strong human ego and yet care for others. We truly believe that he can be a 20/80 person and be a real man without losing anything, and actually gain much by understanding others and his environment much better and make decisions and do actions that are good and healthy.

Most importantly, for all males now and for the future of mankind in general he believes that women are equal in the eyes of God, that they are different but not inferior in any way. Their way of viewing and thinking and their acting with the input of all their senses is just fine and the will of God. That, due to history man's characteristic of narrow-sighted focus in his view of things and women in their broad view of things, together can be one with God and therefore in all ways be companions, making us much better than we could ever be as individuals. He believes that there is no hierarchy between the genders and that there should be no dominance – those days are now past! Therefore, he treats women with respect, he never uses a woman for sexual desires or uses them in any way.

That means that the new person man uses no one and especially he does not use women for use. He loves them as friends, even having women spiritual friends who are close friends that he interacts with without the sexual component that many mistakenly believe is the only way that men and women can interact with one another.

This breaks the false concept that because of male dominance and female subordination they cannot be 20/80 people or friends, let alone be companions.

We can now be companions and the new person man can do this without losing a single thing. In fact, now the female can and will be able to interact with men in a community of honesty, reality, and emotion without the man being compromised in any way. This will help men to be their true selves, cast off the lies of the false self and enter the world that God had made in the Garden!

BEHOLD: THE NEW PERSON WOMAN

Since, our tradition in society was that a woman's greatest value lay in birth and nurturing our species they were "used" for sexual gratification by the male hidden behind the disguise of propagation, protection, and provision. But as noted with this male sexual gratification came protection, and protection for the woman by the male. However, this subordination led to some degree of true organization and property laws that have served us well despite their reason for being. Due to major disruptions in human history such as the great plague in Europe which disrupted land ownership, and in some cases destroyed entire families, the importance of heirship and property ownership helped to provide the woman with importance for the economic reasons noted earlier.

Sometimes marriage was for the true love of a woman by a male. Often it was more a commercial transaction than what all knew it was supposed to be in theory. Different cultures, different variations of this ownership, but much the same story and values.

With the passage of history and we believe in God's time this ownership relationship and the domination and subordination of humans in the "might-makes-right" world has modified some. Or, should I say, should have modified some. Has it changed in reality?

Yes, of course it has changed! Women are able to produce children through science live beyond a few years, women survive pregnancies, work in all capacities in most human civilizations, and are no longer thought of by most of society as just chattel. Women, in general, in society's terms are not as subordinate.

Except, except possibly in the image and persona of the Brutus psyche! And herein lies the problem!

Many of those male characteristics of Brutus we mentioned previously are still in the personas of most males. And that persona's view of women is still pretty much intact.

Men don't like to talk about this and in fact do not talk about this at all cost. Most don't even realize that they feel consciously and subconsciously the need to be and live out this persona. Some may even feel queasy about these types of thoughts, but most don't. This traditional male persona defines them as a man, period. They do not question it. It is the only way to be! It got our world this far, don't mess with it.

Many women of today seem to handle their current relationship with the Brutus male or the Brutus parts of a male by imitating the male and acting like society has taught them to act. She often gives males her soft female characteristics that he desires unless of course she is using them to seduce or deceive him. When this is the situation, she becomes an opponent of the male even if stealth and in competition with him. She even allows this to claim companionship and desire for relationship and community. She embraces radical feminism claiming even the extreme of her right to kill her own children!

But these overt but covert relationships are not based upon love, trust, friendship or community and therefore they do not work!

They are not working and will not work because this is not what God meant for her or mankind!

What God meant for her going forward was to be the progeny of the true mother of mankind, Mary. She is to take her true place as part of mankind and now live in her true nature. She is to be her real self, a woman and proud of it, using all her loving God-like characteristics as:

THE NEW PERSON WOMAN!

What makes a woman this new person woman? How can she not be a molded subordinate as she has always been? Is she to act differently toward herself, the males in her life, society? And, what does that mean? Is it utopia of thought, or is it real? What is she transforming into? Is it even possible? How can she possibly take her weight of sin, the sin of Eve, her unworthiness and make her into what she was meant to be, a Mary, a successful companion of God and man?

She can be who she is truly meant to be, her real self. But she will never succeed by being what she is not, a male. She must be all woman. She must be what God meant for her to be and be glad she is.

This starts where one would expect for it to start and will continue to be:

With God!

To be that new person woman she must be who she is meant to be and conform to her very purpose for being and existing. This FOUNDATION is crucial. She was born with the characteristics of God that are unique to her and allows her to now be God's Helper and man's helper. The FOUNDATION has to do with her belief in who God is and plays out in the world as her faith fulfilling her destiny. That FOUNDATION that is necessary to fulfill her role as the world moves forward is:

- That God is pure love.
- A gut belief that God (Trinity) loves each of us unconditionally, just as we are!

- Some women may tend to believe they are unworthy of God's love. But it seems they can accept that God loves them unconditionally more than they can accept that they are worthy of God's love. Sometimes logic, based on the message of the Bible can help one begin to accept that God is love and that He loves all. If we say God does not love a woman then we seem to state that God is either crazy or a liar. Or, maybe He loves each woman and is telling the truth. The decision is which does the woman believe? Once it is believed that God loves her unconditionally then it may allow her heart to open and begin to accept that she also loves herself.
- That God is the God of the Cosmos for eternity, eternal Creator and always present everywhere at all times.
- That God, Jesus the Christ, has forgiven her/me for my sins.
- If I love myself because God loves me, then I love others because that is what God, as Jesus, the Christ asks of me.
- I do not deliberately defy God, but I sometimes fail God by not loving Him to the degree I should love Him, thus placing a barrier between God and myself that I am responsible for removing.
- That we are made to be in an eternal close relationship with God.
- That Jesus as the Second Person of the Trinity who became one of us, being born of Mary who is a unique human in all of eternity, and who endured everything we endure in our lives as a human. Jesus came to earth for redemption of all sins but also to show us by word and example how we are to love the Trinity, ourselves and our neighbors.
- Success in life is "Living in The Mind of Christ" by being a disciple of Christ in all aspects of living.

And with this as the New Person Woman's Foundation, She Lives in the Mind of Christ through the 20/80 Rule.

This means that she reacts as the new person woman to all others including the male, be he Brutus or the new person man. How does the new person woman do this?

She refers back 2,000 years to the last place she might think of going! MARY! Mary is the model and a helper, Mary, not as a timid woman but as the first disciple of Jesus, the Christ, God Incarnate as a human. She is a strong person, a strong woman. Although Mary is a unique human in all of eternity, she is a woman and we can imitate her behavior, she is one of us remember! As the Marists suggest, Mary is "hidden and unknown", therefore she exercises the 20/80 rule by not emphasizing herself but being focused on the other as if she were "hidden and unknown". More importantly for our discussion she is, "like a bridge" by showing us God's way and being the conduit from God to man and therefore also a conduit or bridge between men and women.

We can learn much from what we can assume of Mary's character and temperament. For women any resistance to Mary is a resistance to her true femininity as a woman since Mary is the epitome of God's femininity. We believe as Catholics that she was born without the stain of Original Sin, instilled with Original Blessing, and was unable to commit sin since Jesus, the Christ, had pre-redeemed her by His sacrifice. Jesus is God and His time is eternal in nature and is not subject to our time limitations. This meant that she would either not see the sinful alternative or she would be aware of the sinful alternative and always dismiss it. She would always choose God's will!

If Mary is the model for the New Person Woman then
Mary always lived in "The Mind of Christ".
So, how would Mary or the New Person
Woman living in The Mind of Christ with
The FOUNDATION deal
with the characteristics of the Brutus or any male?

Since a Brutus type usually brings confrontation with him when he deals with women (domination, subordination, disrespect, power, control, inequality, lack of understanding of how women think and act, etc.) she needs to understand the God-given differences between women and men we have discussed. Further, as a new person woman she must always strive to know herself truthfully, her root causes of sin, her root virtues and she must like who she is with the good and the bad, i.e., she must love herself because God loves her recognizing the faults that challenge her relationship with Him.

With her FOUNDATION of faith, the new person woman can use her model of woman, Mary, in her reaction to the Brutus male characteristics. We will now see how the new person woman deals with characteristics of the Brutus male in the way that Mary teaches her.

> The root cause of this confrontational attitude of Brutus may well be based on his domination characteristic which in turn is based upon his hierarchical focus. Therefore, we are reminded that what this means is that with the woman he will act in the same way he deals with men but even to a greater degree because of his feeling of natural dominance and superiority, i.e., he validates himself by where he sees himself in the hierarchy of all creatures and human society. His ego means he must be one up on others, above them on the hierarchy scale which makes him by nature a very competitive oriented person. He must win and to lose is always negative no matter what the circumstances.

Mary would have encountered the hierarchical male in the same way she dealt with all people. She would have loved him despite his proclivity to domination. She would not have shown any favoritism toward his position and in her reaction to it. She would have been honest and lovingly straightforward in her interface with him. Her responses would be truthful, and her interaction would be an attempt to work with him peacefully and support his efforts if they were warranted, i.e., in line with the will of God. She would not become angry, frustrated or irritated with him; she would engage him in interaction that would promote clarity and be beneficial to both. She would not hesitate to suggest to him the better course of action whether solicited from her or not. She would in all ways live in the 20/80 rule and disregard his myopic self-interest actions and words. There is always a more peaceful way to say anything and Mary would have known and used this relationship approach.

When she is confronted with the Brutus, overall, the new person woman would attempt to minimize conflict. This does not mean that she would buckle-under to the male or allow subordination. The key is not to win but to bring both to a feeling of "win" in consensus regarding any issue.

Potential confrontation of any degree from the smallest to major can be minimized by the new person woman by trying to be aware of who she is talking with and be devoid of supposition. Then she is best to not make any assumptions, comparisons or judgments about the other. This allows the opportunity to focus on his words and actions instead of pre-conceived notions about what he will say and his expected demeanor.

She can tell by his actions and words whether she is dealing with a male with some or all Brutus characteristics or whether she is dealing with a new person man. Either way she will approach the interaction in the same way she would deal with anyone. Just like Mary.

Without sin Mary was able to live the 20/80 rule which means she was able to a greater degree interpret the words and actions of others and discern their motivations, needs, their false selves and their real selves and react in the right way (God's way) accordingly. The new person woman through her natural feminine characteristics sees with a broader view than the male and is capable of better understanding Jesus.

This is where she through her quiet nature and broader senses would naturally be acting in a mode of charitable interpretation, i.e. showing respect for the other even if in complete disagreement with any aspect of his behavior while seeing his orientation and discerning if he is being honest and real or being manipulative. Therefore, she would not compromise him as a person but view him as a child of God no matter how wrong he might be about an issue or how he might be attempting to dominate and force a feeling or command on her. She would be looking for, "the Christ in him" and trying to engage him.

When dealing with a male who believes that women are too emotional, the new person woman need not be devoid of emotion. She, like Mary, will keep her emotions at a level based upon the situation, not upon legacy with the man based upon some other experience. But she does have the responsibility of not allowing herself to use her emotions to manipulate the situation or to blow the whole situation out of reasonable proportions.

One could argue that a new person woman would hold emotions and deal with them in a more extended way than men do. It takes her longer to process through the emotion or emotions developed as a result of an encounter, good or bad. Therefore, she would have to exercise self-restraint in not harboring any ill will just as we would imagine Mary her model would have done.

The new person woman, like Mary, may handle her emotional legacy with the man by bringing her feelings to his attention. The man may not be able to appreciate her emotional holdover or think it makes sense because his emotions come and go due to his narrow focus and he often is "all done" with the situation shortly after it ends.

Her emotions if real and honest will have an effect on him. Despite his false self demeanor he may be moved by her emotional response and her willingness to bring her true emotional situation to his attention. Often women do not do this and harbor resentment against the man because she is still involved in the situation emotionally when he has moved on. Using the gift of self-control by sharing her feelings with him about the situation may soften his heart and hers as well. Often sharing feelings bring the two to a better understanding of one another.

If he shows no interest in her true emotions, then she knows what kind of male she is dealing with and she will chalk it up to his failure at this moment in the relationship and realize this area of incompatibility. This implies that she, as the new person woman with Mary as her model, follows by choosing to forgive and not harbor a grudge.

It may be very important that the new person woman explains to the man why her reaction is emotional instead of not providing any explanation and just harboring an internal grudge. This explanation allows the man to understand that there is logic behind her emotion generated by his words and actions. This allows him to understand her reason for her emotion and possibly helps him to soften his heart so he can understand her better. This opens the door to charitable interpretation. Of course, the man needs to be willing to listen and the woman needs to be willing to explain her emotional state to him each and every time.

In dealing with anyone but especially in dealing with the male, especially the Brutus male, the new person woman must be who she is without compromise. She knows that God loves her unconditionally, she loves herself and by her very nature she is inclined to love others. It is her nature. That nature cannot be compromised or shown disrespect by anyone. But she cannot enforce that brutally. She knows God's will for her as did Mary and she must live it out with others as did Mary.

Companions?

In light of, what has been said think how did Mary interacted with Joseph, friends, family and neighbors? How did Mary discipline Jesus, how did she talk with and to Him? With anyone you may be sure she lived the old adage, "hate the sin but love the sinner". She probably always saw the sin, showed compassion for the sinner, but always knew that the only action was to do the will of God. This is why Mary and why our new person woman is here!

We might be reminded that Mary without sin and always cognizant of her environment and those in it knew what to say when and where. She spoke at Cana when her words were important for the moment and for eternity and she did not speak at the foot of the cross when the key person in all of eternity spoke for Himself and her and only her presence was needed to represent you and me. So, Mary's mission was to do God's Will only to the best of her ability and she spoke in ways that would be pleasing to God to bring peace and blessings to all relationships. She spoke truth in love, compassion and mercy not in anger, revenge or selfishness. So, as a new person woman she desires to imitate her as she encounters the Brutus male and/or anyone.

So, Mary's interaction and the new person woman's interaction with a man should be the same at all times, what God meant for Adam and Eve, what He meant for men and women, companionship! She is the helper of Adam, she is the one that makes the companionship and brings them into common, makes it work, makes them whole.

Within the interaction with the male the new person woman truly becomes this helper of the male. As we have said very often, his tendency is immediate reaction due to a narrow focus. She on the other hand breathes in, accesses the situation, listens to her instincts, evaluates the situation, considers all the parties involved, and with him they have a common companionship in the decision/solution facing them. She does not necessarily do this too slowly although it may take her longer than the knee jerk reaction of the male, but she takes in the situation with all of her senses and does not wait too long if a situation decries an immediate response.

What about her immediate jerky emotion? The man's immediate reaction in dualistic mind frame is based on his limited logical perception. Which would be devoid of the many senses of the woman looking at it. Let us be clear, in certain situations a decision may need to be made quickly or the male's emotions are not as involved as the woman's and therefore his ability to decide quickly is a wonderful gift and appreciated by the woman. By contrast the woman in her immediate reaction might immediately draw upon emotion with crying – raised voice, becoming irrational, angry or overly emotionally involved. This may be her first response or her emotional response but she is as capable as the male is to make logical and solid decisions.

If she perceives he is reacting in some way that leads to an action too quickly and does not take into consideration everything that should be taken-in, then she in her role can help calm him down without injuring his ego. Why be cruel when you can be kind.

What does this do for the male? It helps him to listen to her and keeps him from making too quick a decision. This allows the woman to build up a frame of reference with him that he will trust in a repetitive way. This helps to break down the idea in the Brutus male that women are slow thinkers and can't seem to "make a decision". They just get there a different way and mitigate as a companion for a better response.

This supposed delay on the part of the woman if perceived as a negative, begs the question of the difference in perception by the male and the female. Mary and any woman by nature looks at things broadly and uses all her senses in reaction. Her God-like characteristics and use of her senses to praise God makes sense to Christians who believe that we are to love God with all of our senses as well as with, "heart, mind, and soul". Some Christians are uncomfortable praising God with all of their senses.

How would Mary or a new person woman deal with her inherent difference in view and response between women and men? As we noted earlier there is often no time restraint for her and her companionship in trying to help the male look at the broader picture that includes emotions, the individuals involved, a true scope of any issue positive or negative and then trying to focus on all aspects coming to a common companionship answer. This nullifies dominance, provides better solutions to any problems and teaches the male the potential problem with his narrow-focused dualism. The woman's influence and the natural way she can get the attention of the male often allows him to look at things more broadly as she does without his loss of ego.

To highlight the root cause of the Brutus's false self the Brutus is extremely egotistical and self-centered. To many, the root of all sin is egoism and self-centeredness. How does the new person woman deal with a man who is extremely egotistical and self-centered? Cannot an issue be handled well if a person is egotistical and self-centered and if not, why? After all, often this motivation produces a decision that is right in the eyes of God. But it is arrived at by Brutus with the wrong motivation, the motivation being selfish and not including what is best for the other. It is all "me".

One problem with Brutus in this regard is he can't see the ramifications of his decisions. Since his evaluation is always what is best for him, even if the action helps others at the same time, this is not his focus or motivation. Information is given to him and disregarded, he discounts everything, and then he decides. His result goes way beyond the possibility of another option being true and is tuned out and even if a decision may be wrong and hurt others it does not matter to him because he is not willing to listen and receive another's view.

And since he is not willing to listen to others then who is he really listening to? He will only rely on himself, his ego, which is all he thinks he needs. However, how can he be sure that his unwillingness to consider others might mean he is listening to more than his ego – maybe the evil one or to some person who has been a predominant negative influence in his life or even his subconscious. Listening to yourself and not wanting to listen to others is where one may do harm.

How would Mary deal with such an egocentric male?

She (and the new person woman) would rely on her broad range of senses to do her evaluation of the situation in "woman time" disregarding what she might assume to be the Brutus response whether immediate or in her legacy view of the male. Her responsibility to herself and the male is to voice her opinion in a consultative way. That is not done through confrontation or anger! Her best strategy would be to move toward a companion solution through an "if/then" conversation pointing out various aspects of the situation that she has discerned and provide these to the male in a spirit of helpfulness. She would make the issue not "his issue" but "their issue" without dictating her approach or solution as the right and only view.

She may even express to him how women think as a way of establishing her right to be respected by the male and be allowed to have a real voice. The advantage for him, obvious or not to him, is her way of looking at the issue may differ from his or confirm his as well as provide the confirmation to his ego.

She is fostering companionship. Her actions are helping him to be more conducive to companionship – maybe showing him her heart, affection, love, emotion can cut down a wall he thinks he must have. She must let him know that winning does not impress her. It may impress "them". i.e. someone else. Let him know he is important in your life and that it is okay when he lets you into his life. Get to the point, "if you fail in some things in life, I will still have respect for you". I will care for you with my female characteristics. This is reality, this is love, this is Mary!

She must clear her head and possess the ability to tell a man what the result is of his actions being egotistically or self-consciously motived and what could happen or would happen in a given situation, helping him understand why they are companions. If he does not want the companionship or the help, you best see the red flag that has gone up. The new person woman can try but, ultimately, she cannot control the other's behavior.

If she can do so in the right or loving way she can basically be telling him, "look buddy, i.e. my companion, not listening to me and not talking with me might make you look bad due to a bad decision that you made without me but if we are companions our companioned action will be ours and not just yours to bear the burden alone". If you exclude me because of disrespect for me or your own prejudices and you don't listen or talk to me as a confidant then we are probably not compatible. Then I need to understand why!

In this type of situation, a woman would be wise to know what a man's relationship with God is and his view of women. She will also want to understand why we are equal yet different? Tell me who a real man is and how he must act to be a real man? You may think that you are everything a woman wants in your head and to you I may look good to other men in your view with me on your arm but if you cannot answer these questions like a real man, then to me you may not be one. I am a companion. I am not a tool of your ego to be used for your own selfish reasons. I may very well say "no" to you because if I cannot be your companion then I have no place as you see it in your life, and I want nothing less. That is exactly what God had in mind! This is a new person woman living in the "mind of Christ".

To look at another Brutus characteristic, Brutus is often looked upon as being Stoic in demeaner and character. Being stoic is defined as one being free of passion, unmoved by joy or grief, and one that submits without complaining to unavoidable necessity. He does not complain and believes that if he shows his emotions and does not guard his feelings he will be viewed by others as a weak man. He is the Marlboro man!

Few males are really stoics. They are mainly using it as an exterior gesturing to suppress a fear of showing emotion and compassion.

However, it takes little effort to see the connection of this stoic image to Brutus and many males of today. In short, in this writing, he is stoic to live the life of his false self, not his real self. He wishes to be stoic to the outer world but inside it creates turmoil. However, the influence of the woman in any capacity of relationship with him may crack this stoic exterior as he interiorly yearns to be free to express emotion and other feelings.

The New Person Woman will help this stoic male heal the wounds of his real self and allow him to express emotions without judgment due to her silent loving support and her gentle dialogue. Just being there with him may allow him to talk about things privately without her speaking – simply listening may go far. She should be herself and completely honest about who she is complete with emotions. This can make a positive impression on him which may allow him to begin to be more comfortable with emotion and believe that it is okay to show emotion. She can even help him to see the value and blessing of tears at appropriate times. The more he is shown emotion in any venue that she might take him or as he runs up against it in real life the more it becomes okay and the easier for him to show his emotions.

Showing compassion by a male is not the rule since winning or losing gives no room for compassion for the one who loses. He has failed in the eyes of all and does not deserve compassion. Surrendering, i.e. losing is very difficult for males since males are to win regardless of the odds. She can help him understand that winning or losing, he is still acceptable and loved. He must learn that being compassionate as a man is a freedom given to him to exercise.

The new person woman can help a man with this characteristic by teaching him compassion by demonstrating for him and others – the only way you live your life. Compassion toward pets, children, hurting adults, hungry people, him, and being a good Samaritan in her life can often chip away at his "win at all cost" orientation. By her actions she can help him to move to believing that being compassionate is a characteristic of a real male who has the freedom to show care for anyone or anything less fortunate.

As suggested earlier the most unfortunate factor in the relationship between women and men is that there is a propensity in our society to be violent toward women. Through what is really "mental rape" some men psychologically abuse women, some men even still beat, rape and kill women, often the one's they claim to love. Even in supposedly good marriages there is too often psychological abuse and physical abuse.

What can a new person woman learn from Mary about how to handle a man that might be prone to abuse her in any way? First, she should not enter any relationship with any man she suspects might be prone to harm her psychologically or physically! If she is in such a relationship, she should get out of it! Secondly, if there are children, she should remove them from this relationship!

If she has not experienced these forms of violence, she knows a woman who has experienced them! She must always be true to her spiritual foundation. Mary would have been. However, at this point she must be honest with herself and understand the realities of the situation and act accordingly. The more complicated the relationship in terms of children, property, etc.... the more she must realize who she is really dealing with and be willing to end the relationship.

Harsh actions but necessary! With her innate fear of men due to their physical superiority it will be hard enough for her to love a man in the way that God meant for her to love him. She may be able to put up with certain Brutus characteristics, but she must protect her life physically and psychologically above all from abuse in any form.

There are good men, new person men who will not treat her that way. But even the new person woman, with the legacy of abuse in the back of her mind, may be able to unconditionally love her children but may be challenged to try to love a man unconditionally in the way God meant for her to love him.

We think Mary would be a model for a woman who would be willing to establish the relationships of any kind with a man who would be the man God meant for him to be – a man who never harms a woman in any way!

Therefore, the new person woman must be careful of her relationships. She must always be straight forward and as honest as possible with everyone, including the male (men) in her life and including herself.

There is a challenge before all parents and particularly women in this regard and in man/woman relationships and that is how do we raise young women to be new persons, i.e., the relationship with God and with the unique characteristics He has given to women to help women have equality and feel that they are worthy individuals.

We suggest that we should teach girls at the earliest age to:

- Know the real God, which is a God of love, not judgment, not condemning.
- Know God loves them just as they are forever physically, emotionally, intellectually, spiritually and any other way.
- That God is always with them.
- That God is always forgiving them.

- That they have more of the characteristics of God than the male.
- They are worthy of God's love.
- That they can have a more intimate relationship with God than a male and she is conduit for an intimate relationship with God for the male.
- That the evil one perpetuates the male dominated foundation of society.
- She is the companion of the male, not subordinate or inferior but different.
- She is different from the male and that is good with those differences being associated with her being more like God.
- That she is equal to the male in all but physical strength.
- Mary is her model.
- God's gift of technology has freed her to be the new person woman and the companion of the male.
- She must be loved in total by the male – anything less is not acceptable.
- She must be respected by all as an equal human being.

"You is kind. You is smart. You is important." *"The Help" Kathryn Stockett*

"Like Wonder Woman the superhero, and Mary, Woman of Wonder, we do battle with the forces of evil. We triumph not with fists or firepower, but with submission to the superhuman power of grace. Mary shows us that a woman who does it well reflects the rightful dignity of a true and powerful feminine mystique that carries great spiritual weight. I am a woman of wonder. I must go first." *(The Wonder of Woman Sonja Corbitt The Great Adventure Blog 4-20-2016)*

BEHOLD: AM I A "COMPANION AT LAST?"

AM I "A NEW PERSON"?

What is necessary for men and women to become companions? We suggest that in order to become companions as discussed here both must want to be new persons and are on paths trying to become new persons.

Let us be clear – it may not be possible for both to be new persons all the time nor at the same time, but we should strive to do so. Relationships have their trying times as well as their joyous times. But the key word is "try" to be a new person all of the time.

Without the characteristics of a new person it is very hard for one to be oriented toward the other in the way that God asks us to be in a close personal relationship such as marriage and spiritual friendship.

There is no room for God within us if we are filled with our false selves.

Therefore, the new person will start with the proper perspective of the real characteristics of God/Trinity as seen in the Bible and in Tradition. We must embrace the 20/80 rule and live the rule day in and day out within the Mind of Christ. These two will give us the FOUNDATION of faith and faith exercised in life that is necessary to be a companion of another.

As we have discussed the Christian God is the God (Trinity) of the Cosmos which allows us to understand that all that goes on in our Cosmos for all time, be it human or non-human is created and ultimately controlled by God. This God is a God of complete and ultimate love and yearns for relationship with each of us which is our ultimate reason for being. Through free will we choose to give up control of our lives to God and to love God and love our neighbor, or not to. If not, then we take on what will be the ultimate failure of trying to be God which is not our true nature or reason for existence.

If we accept our ultimate reason for existence, then we are part of a love relationship with God through the Holy Spirit that allows us to accept and love ourselves just as we are as well as love God in return and love others. We then have the truth of our goodness and our ability to love ourselves and others. This is the foundation of companionship and it cannot exist without this divine and human orientation.

With this acceptance there is no confusion about how we are to love others. Gone is the idea that in order to love others we must deny ourselves completely. We must love and embrace who we are with the acceptance that we are aware of the good and not so good characteristics. To lie about ourselves and who we are or to think that we cannot be ourselves creates the false self or a lie. Then, by nature we will be dishonest and not in companionship with anything. That does not mean we cannot improve ourselves, but we must be very clear in who we are so that we can mitigate our characteristics that keep us from loving as we should ourselves, God and others. To have God in control does not release us of our responsibilities to put the realities about God and His creation into action.

But our focus cannot be so on ourselves that our biggest possible sin takes control, i.e., an inflated ego and self-centeredness. The 20/80 rule helps us to keep the proper balance between our necessary and healthy ego and our ability to love God and others. A healthy ego needs for us to spend 20% of ourselves on ourselves to insure we are who we are, who we can be, and improve ourselves as human beings. But to love others we must allow 80% of ourselves to love others, i.e., knowing others, who they are, what is motivating them, why they are saying or doing what they are doing, how they are hurting, how they are loving, etc. without the interference or judgement of our own personal outside factors influencing us with our own prejudices that interfere with the ability to love and serve others. Yes, serve others. That is a part of loving! Without judgement, prejudice or exception!

These two approaches, the spiritual FOUNDATION and the 20/80 rule moves our thoughts away from just ourselves and on to a communion of thought that has God as its foundation and the love of ourselves clearly in the right quantity with the love of others. The two approaches foster and are necessary for companionship to exist. The result:

THIS IS THE NEW PERSON READY FOR COMPANIONSHIP

In the ultimate example of companionship as in a marriage it is advantageous that we understand that the companionship between a woman and a man consists of new persons. If one in the marriage is not a new person then the purity aspect or the protection aspect is not at the epitome God intended. If the male is not a new person, he is not "protecting" the purity of the woman which is innate, and a God demanded responsibility. There can be no companionship, only hierarchical relationship when the new person characteristics are missing. To abdicate God given responsibilities in loving the whole woman on the part of the man or surrendering of the whole woman on the part of the woman, then commitment to the complete love element in the relationship is not protection and is not purity. We are not defining terms in a secular dictionary. We are defining terms in God's dictionary! That is why a non-new person relationship of one of the parties cannot be a Trinitarian Communion marriage. The new person must seriously through prayer and guidance determine if they are doing God's will, because in essence they may be only "using the other".

Since the grace of the Trinity through the Holy Spirit comes to each person in God's time many respond to God at a later point in life and become new persons with a legacy other than that of the new person. As a man is given the new sight through grace, he may have compromised his innate male role of protector of her purity or she may have compromised the purity of the companionship. Falling on their knees they ask for cleansing and renewal through the ever-forgiving Christ and the reconciliation of his body on earth, the Church. Then, as Paul they pick themselves up from the ground and they live new as the new person in the wonderful joy of grace given in the immeasurable flow of love from the Trinity. With grace the purity of the woman and the purity of the companionship will be restored to their psyches and souls allowing them to move forward, no longer as slaves or slavers but lovers – as God meant for them to be!

BEHOLD: AM I A "COMPANION AT LAST?"

AM I SELF-CENTERED?

It is very hard to be disordered when being self-centered and be a new person. A healthy ego results in a mental feeling of well-being when viewing ourselves, who we are and who we are not, our ability to assay ourselves as being okay if not perfect and being our own master. This is easier said than done and psychological problems develop when any one of these areas is distorted or disoriented. We are influenced by many things in life and chiseled by many experiences good and bad. Spiritually, again we may turn to Saint Ignatius of Loyola whose gift of understanding human nature tells us that we must know ourselves, our virtues and vices and understand how influences in life can place us into periods of consolation and desolation. Why go to Ignatius? Because our concerns are spiritual in nature involving ourselves in relation to the Trinity, ourselves, and our fellow man and he had important spiritual insight into these areas.

Inspired by St. Ignatius of Loyola what might be the questions to ask ourselves about our being too self-centered:

- What are my fears?
- Do I have a view of God as a Being to be feared or loved?
- Does this Being love me or is He dualistic and waiting for me to fail in some way?
- Do I fear that I am bad by design and cannot really do better?
- Do I fear others?

- Am I in competition with all others?
- Do I have to win to be ok?
- Do I have to be successful in power, or money or both to show others that God has favored me?
- Do I have to feel good about myself and show my pride to all?
- Do I compare myself with others based on man's criteria?
- Am I scrupulous?
- Do I think that I am the one in control?
- How do I respond to criticism or negative comments?
- Am I dualistic?
- Am I overly defensive?
- Is the Trinity a close friend?
- Is God Abba to me?
- Where is God to me and when?
- Do I have a problem with a 20/80 rule?
- Do I think God wants it to be a 0/100 rule?
- If I fail in life will anyone love me?
- Do we focus on the negative qualities of others versus focusing on their positive qualities?

Our responses to the questions may suggest that we may be too self-centered, too preoccupied with ourselves to focus much on others unless, of course, they fulfill our personal need, or I can use them to obtain a happy answer to one of these questions. The spiritual and psychological reality is that when we think of the other 80% of the time, we ourselves become happier individuals and more well-adjusted. Maybe this is part of the living in the Mind of Christ, i.e., doing God's will and fulfilling the purpose and existence that God has given us as humans on this earth and me as an individual. And, oh by the way, the other applies to humans and nonhumans. Nature cannot sin and go against God's will. It does not have free will. We do. Genesis tells us we have the responsibility for others (Cain and Abel) and we have responsibility for nature and all the Cosmos. That is if we can move beyond our nose to care for others. We need the

20% to love ourselves but we need all the other 80% to love the others created by God.

So then, living in our male dominant society, what is our hierarchy now?

We have said that we do everything the male way. That means hierarchy. Then what should that male way be when we are dealing with spiritual matters as Christians?

All would answer, "God first". But if that is our answer then we are indeed right but that must be shown in how we actually love our God, ourselves, and others (man and nature). Are we 20/80 or somewhere else?

As a new person we should put God first, then ourselves, then others. That is the hierarchy, but it must be 20/80. Who do I report to? Who determines if I am successful? How is success defined? If I fail is it ok? Jesus showed that "the down was the top", "the servant, the true master", "the failed, the successful". As a new person and wanting-to-be disciples of Christ and wishing to live in the mind of Christ - do our answers conform with His or is our rule something other than the 20/80 rule? As a new person I must look at moving from my self-centered nature to a nature that is the new person.

BEHOLD: AM I A "COMPANION AT LAST?"

CAN I LOSE?

Do I lose as a male in being the new person? Can anyone lose by being the new person? Since men are competitive by nature and loss is failure to many males then it begs the question! Of course, the question is also very important to women because often when men lose, women lose also in the primary way but also in many other ways. No one likes to lose!

But what is loss? Losing depends on how you assay your issues in life and how you define success and who you are and who you have to be successful to. What is losing in man's economy is not necessarily a loss in God's economy. Therefore, losing for the new person can be winning!

If we measure success by winning over another in a fair and competitive way, then that may be a quite valid win. However, if that win is based upon ego only and only on our side of our nose then maybe it is not a win. Because a new person measures success and winning only in the realm of God's economy. If I destroy my opponent and win and cause harm to him/her in the process, then I have lost as a new person. Winning is defined by the new person to be found only in the building up of relationships and community, never in the diminutive effect or destruction of either. The result of winning is a feeling of well-being, happiness, joy, peace and being in community with others and our environment, mitigating confrontation, being in God's wisdom and exercising self-control.

THEN AND ONLY THEN DO YOU WIN – YOU WILL NEVER EVER LOSE!

YOU NEVER LOSE DOING THE WILL OF GOD!

MEASURE YOUR SUCCESS IN THE CONTEXT OF ETERNITY, NOT WHAT WILL MAKE YOU ONE-UP ON YOUR FELLOW MAN TODAY!

We can ask ourselves, what does this interaction, situation, challenge, etc. have for me and compare that to what can I get from God? What I might get for me is often transitory – winning, success, happiness, stroking my ego and maybe at the expense of others, etc. What I might get from winning in God's economy might be a continuous feeling of well-being and happiness and building up the Kingdom of God. The better question is, what can I give God in this interaction, situation, challenge, etc.? That's "win", that is when I WIN!

When I win the way of a new person wins! I help secure the Body of Christ! When I fail to be the new person, when I am on my own side of my nose when I have to be one up on my fellow man/woman then I may well be headed into sin and compromising my relationship with the Trinity. Then I have just taken a brick out of the brick wall that is the Church, the Body of Christ, Christ on Earth. Therefore, my actions in serving myself only has lessened the strength of the wall that is the Body of Christ and made it weaker. As a new person when I see this happen as a result of my pride then I must restore my relationship with my fellow man that I have degraded and restore my relationship with God, both in the context of forgiveness. This allows my brick to be placed back into the wall which results in it only being strengthened.

Will this happen to a new person? Of course, we are not perfect as we have said earlier but we all have the ability and responsibility to "try". Therefore, in our trying, working on replacing our brick in the wall, we are encouraged and are an example to others to continue to try and try and try again.

As a note on this my fellow readers what we are not saying is that you should not have a strong ego. That 20/80 rule takes seriously the 20% ego part. We must love ourselves because God loves us. But we have no right to do so by walking on the bodies of others to enhance our own self-centeredness. This is not a healthy ego. This is the Brutus, be him a man or a woman!

WE ARE NEW PERSON WOMEN AND MEN!

BEHOLD: AM I A "COMPANION AT LAST?"

DO I THINK THIS IS REAL?

Why would it not be real? If being, i.e., acting as a new person everyday was not realistic then for this man this change in behavior suggested would not be possible and we have wasted a lot of paper. Or, if the world were not changing then the Brutus persona would be working well in the world. If Jesus, the Christ had not been real then we would have no model for the actions needed by a new person man. If Mary were not who she really was then the new person woman would have no model of how to deal with a Brutus or any male.

But we maintain that Jesus, the Christ was fully man/fully God and is a doable model for all men. We believe that Brutus is no longer helpful in a no-longer "might-makes" right world that is rapidly fading if not already passé.

So, is being the new person doable? Yes, the 20/80 rule gives us a daily goal. St. Ignatius gives us what we need to own-up with honesty about ourselves which gives us the virtues we need to use and the personal rat holes we need to avoid. We need to know who we are and accept it and then "try" to be aware of how we might react to any situation confronting us. We need to have the foundation of knowing and believing in our gut that God loves us unconditionally, that He is complete love beyond our understanding, that He has forgiven us through His becoming a human like us, that we in turn must love Him by trying to show our love for him by not hurting others and not turning our back through actions on Him, and that we try to love others despite our prejudices and their difficulties. That if we are a man we understand the differences in us given to women by God, that we respect who they are, that they are to be loved as equals sent to man to help man know God, that they are our companions and that we should never ever "use" them. And, they, women, must in turn fulfill the companion role given to them by God in the Garden and now in the reality of our age and the ages to come and that their model is Mary who has been there for all of us as a guide to discipleship with the Christ.

It being real has a wonderful payoff of each of us being in harmony with all others and things and of a feeling of comfort in who we are and why we are here and where we will be going.

These are the fruits of companionship!

BEHOLD: AM I A "COMPANION AT LAST?"

AM I WILLING TO BE A COMPANION DURING CONFLICT?

Conflicts between only two adult individuals occur at several different levels. They occur between two individuals such as a man and a woman with frequency in most of our lives. A conflict or more possibly labeled a disagreement may be mild and short lived. It may happen so spontaneously and resolved so quickly that we often do not really retain the memory of the occurrence. However, even the mildest conflict may be retained in our memory since conflicts usually have a winner and a looser. This may be especially true in incidents that are mild and short in duration. Too many of these mild but short occurrences in which we either win or lose may lay over time in our memory and if we are often the winner or the looser we build up a certain frame of reference regarding dealing with the specific other that may adversely affect the relationship. Someone wins, but, and it is a big "but", someone also loses.

Other legacy involvement with the other may also affect the instance of conflict with information that is outside and possibly irrelevant to the instance. We may be preloaded to disagree with the other based upon past instances. If a conflict is more than superficial then the stakes may be higher and so is any legacy conflict exchange and preconceived notions regarding the other. In more severe conflicts the results can be harmful to the continued relationship. Usually the severity of the conflict and therefore the win or loss is magnified, the length of the disagreement is prolonged well beyond its rational timeframe and may not really be resolved. It may just be pushed out or submerged in our minds with a residual of harm toward the other that may go on for a long period of time or even for years.

In its most severe form, the conflict may lead to a very damaged if not terminated relationship often disproportionate to the issue being argued.

To act as though conflict should not be part of life is not realistic. But that does not give license to letting conflict become harmful to the existence nor quality of any relationship. But how is it possible if one wins or loses that harmony can exist in a conflict situation? It truly is a zero/sum game for most of us and we are hurt in some way when our score is "zero"!

As a new person trying to be Christ to others and doing God's will of "loving thy neighbor as we love ourselves" how do we handle these spontaneous instances of conflict as well as those who are more severe and of longer duration? How do we level the playing field so that the probability of being the winner or the looser is mitigated and we have a better probability of resolving the instance with as little if no harm to the relationship?

There is no third-party judge or others to pass judgement on the situation and designate a winner and loser. We are not dealing with legal proceedings here. We are dealing with two individuals who have conflict. Again, how do we level the playing field before things begin to get out of hand? How do we lessen the impact of legacy on both sides? Notice the "how do we lessen" these affects right up front in the conflict before it worsens which it will if the duration of the conflict increases? How do we lessen the animosity between the two individuals? How do arguments become discussions instead of arguments?

We would suggest that the "lessening" in the conflict can start with an agreement/commitment on the part of both to begin the conflict resolution process by always, always, always beginning exactly in the same way no matter how angry or emotional we might be at the moment. This requires an agreement to this resolution process up front before any conflict occurs. Wow is that possible? Of course, it is possible! If you are on the path trying to seriously live as the new person you can. But even if only one new person will agree beforehand that one new person can act just as if both are in agreement. If the other is not a new person then the new person acts as though both are new persons anyway. No excuses, no outs in responsibility by the new person. "Blessed are the peace makers"!

No one will lose in this up-front process unless you have to win no matter what and you are willing to damage and/or destroy the relationship to get your way. If this is the case, then the relationship does not really exist.

The Steps in Conflict Resolution:

1. Briefly separate from one another, e.g., get a drink of water, go to the restroom or other brief separation. This will help to dissipate the emotion. This allows both to walk-away, then re-engage.
2. Make this happen even if both don't want it: Kneel anywhere (best in a church but not necessary) at any time. Hold hands and pray, "Holy Trinity, allow the two of us to work as companions, i.e., become one in the resolution of this matter. We are committed to the Resolution of this matter and will abide by the Resolution. Neither will win or lose. Amen." Touching helps to reconnect with the other and dissipate emotion. This is a chance through physical contact to start anew together.
3. While still holding hands, one begins to tell their side of the story. They may say whatever for 5 minutes if it takes that long.

The other must remain silent. The one speaking may show emotion but must act in a civil way.
4. The other now tells their side of the story for 5 minutes if it takes that long. The other must remain silent. The one speaking may show emotion but must act in a civil way.
5. Then each says to the other, "I believe that you are sincere in what you have said, and I believe it to be true from your view and said in a vain of true belief. I know you are not trying to manipulate me or lie to me concerning your position on this matter. If I were you, I might believe the same way you do.
6. Then each tells the other individually without interruption by the other what they are willing to give up to the other concerning the matter and what they cannot give up.
7. Arrive at a compromise or agree to disagree as an outcome.
8. The Resolution should be one where neither wins, nor loses and both agree that this is the best they can do. The process should be worked at until that Resolution is found.
9. Ask God to bless the Resolution. Pray Our Father together and then cease to hold hands if wanted.
10. Resolve the situation.

THE BEGINNING OF CHANGE

Or should we say going back to the garden?

The change starts with me as a man or a woman. The old idea "if you want to change the world then start by changing yourself" is true and requires us to put some effort into ourselves so we impact others. So, if we actively work on changing ourselves becoming who God intended us to be, then effectively we change the world around us. The impact we have can be positive or negative depending on another's perspective, but the fact is we believe we are positively being transformed and this positivity feeds our desire to love, praise, honor and serve God.

And as individuals desiring to be in relationship with God and others, we understand that not only do we need to become New Persons but so do those around us. This realization and the effort to change increases our desire to attempt to live by the 20/80 rule. Women and men are equal in the eyes of God but different for a purpose! And, we have grown to understand that men and women are different in many ways. No longer is the might-makes-right world pertinent. No longer is male domination required to survive. Technology as a gift from God neutralizes the Brutus persona and mitigates the disordered ego assisting Brutus in walking step by step to become a new person. As he becomes a new person and as the woman as well transforms to the new person the relationships between the two become more that of companions versus a relationship of competition.

This is our future if we participate, this is who God meant for us to be in relationship with ourselves, others and Him. The choice is ours. The journey is a mixed bag of rough and rugged, smooth and sailing, heartache and heart joy, intellectual understanding as well as intellectual confusion, feelings of defeat and feelings of victory. A journey to the interior of who we are either spiritually or personally is long and hard, it is a journey of a lifetime. This journey is similar to training for and running a marathon race.

One must do the physical work to run that distance, one must do the interior work to run the distance with themselves, others and God.

As the world changes we are reminded that it is God's will that prevails for the future. His will is for us all to be in companionship, this is our legacy, this is our future, this is what God had in mind.

If the purpose of the universe is for men to spend eternity with God, why has the second coming of Christ not happened? Is life to be eternal of this planet? Is the new earth and the new heaven this earth in this universe refined or is there to be a new heaven and a new earth somewhere else? Is the evolution of man then a spiritual evolution after the physical evolution begun by the soul being placed in the body by God? Is spiritual evolution the real evolution, transforming man into what he was meant to be in the Garden? Is the end of evolution to spend eternity with God in the whole universe?

Where is Christianity headed? God's time is not our time, so we of course have no idea of the length of history. Are we the one's to begin the track to the new heaven and the new earth that Jesus is making ready for us?

We know the end. We are just challenged to bring it about by doing our part in our generation. The war is over with evil but the battle leading to that end is still going on.

As Paul stated in 2 Timothy 4:7-8, NRSV "I have fought the good fight, I have finished the race; I have kept the faith. From now on there is reserved for me the crown of righteousness, which the Lord, the righteous judge, will give me on that day, and not only to me, but also to all who have longed for his appearing.

THIS IS WHAT GOD MEANT FOR IT TO BE!

IN CONVERSATION

Sherri: *"Wow what a trip!!"*

Bob: "Well, Sherri, is it doable and is it real?"

Sherri: *"It is doable as long as we have Jesus and Mary as our foundation for being the new person and both as models of love, and for companionship. It also is real."*

Bob: "Sherri, what in our personal experience confirms to us this is real?"

Sherri: *"Well in our relationship we have experienced learning to be new persons. As you know sometimes, we have our disagreements and are highly irritated with one another. However, we have made a commitment as friends that we will live the 20/80 rule. And as co-authors we strive to come to a consensus in our writing because what matters to us is relationship, community and companionship, the credentials of a new person. We as Spiritual Directors know that the journey with God is not an easy one, but it is one that is worth our efforts."*

Bob: "Sherri, I am excited about the changes that God has for the world and how we are positioned in the beginning of these changes. It may be difficult at times, but we already know the end game and the end game is that God wins out with His love of the Cosmos and everyone in it."

Appendix

Is our Relationship - Symmetrical or Asymmetrical?

The Purpose and How to Use the Questionnaire

The purpose of the questionnaire:

This exercise is to be done with your spouse or loved one.

* A litmus test of the effort to become a New Person living in The Mind of Christ.

* How close am I in my thinking of being a New Person?

* In relationship to our loved one how compatible are we in being new persons together?

Help us to realize topics that possibly need discussion either in our personal relationship with God and/or others.

* Possible discussion to consider is how are we progressing as we transform into New Persons and in our relationship with our loved one?

How to use the questionnaire:

The male and the female should each separately:

* Each person should ask the other person the question and evaluate their answer based upon their own criteria of what their view of the answer should be.
* Answer each question using a scale of 1- 10 and place in proper score column.
* Do not discuss the topic of any question until the questionnaire is complete.
* After completion of questionnaire there will be a list of topics for discussion.
* An unwillingness to answer a question at all by the other person means a score of "0".
* Any major disparity between the questioner and the person answering the question might be the subject of discussion but no scores should be changed as a result of the discussion.

Relationship - Symmetrical or Asymmetrical?
(Verbal Exchange - man and woman have their own scores)

Answer each question using a scale of 1-10 and place in proper score column.

Questions

#	Questions for Each Person	Female Score	Male Score
1	Tell me about God?		
2	Where is God?		
3	Are you of the same faith as the other?		
4	Tell me about men?		
5	Tell me about women?		
6	Tell me about who you are?		
7	What is the most mystifying thing about men?		
8	What is the most mystifying thing about women?		
9	What 1 question do you most want to ask men about?		
10	What 1 question do you most want to ask women about?		
11	Do you have a personal relationship with God?		
12	Do you feel unworthy?		
13	Do you need a member of the opposite sex in your life to be happy?		
14	Do you believe in heaven?		
15	Do you believe in hell?		
16	Do you think that men and women are different?		
17	How are men different from women?		
18	How are women different from men?		
19	Name 3 priorities in life in order?		
20	Do you want children?		
21	What is the objective of your sex life?		
22	Do you try to practice the 20/80 % rule?		
23	What 1 group of people do you not like?		

24 Do you attend church every Sunday if you are able to?
25 Tell me about how we "use another"?
26 Who is responsible for raising children?
27 Do you pray each day other than at meals?
28 Do you believe in abortion?
29 Have you ever been arrested?
30 Do you have a best friend?
31 Is the other person doing this questionnaire your friend?
32 Do you allow the other to have a voice? How?
33 Will you share with the other in making financial decisions?
34 What will you not be able to give the other?
35 Do you know I am not your savior?
36 Do you have a good relationship with your parents?
37 Are you separated from a family member or friend? Why?
38 What would you like most about a new person man?
39 What would you like most about a new person woman?
40 Is God a redemptive God or a loving God?
41 How much alcholol do you drink during a week?
42 Do you use illegal drugs?
43 Do you believe in divorce?
44 Will God forgive you for your sins? Has he forgiven you?
45 Do you think you act differently around the other sex?
46 Are you willing to communicate often with the other?
47 Is there any subject you will not discuss with the other?
48 Are you willing to open yourself up to the other?
49 Do you have a problem with intimacy?
50 Can you talk about intimacy?

51 How do you define sin?
52 Will you agree to a method for ending conflict with the other?
53 Are you willing to see a counselor with the other if necessary?
54 Tell me when you must have your way?
55 Are you more of an introvert or an extrovert?
56 Is there something in the other you want to change?

Total

BIBLIOGRAPHY

Robert A. Johnson, Inner Work, Using Dreams and Active Imagination for Personal Growth (Harper One, 1986).

Robert A. Johnson, She, Understanding Feminine Psychology (Harper, 1989).

Robert A. Johnson, He, Understanding Masculine Psychology (Harper Perennial, 1989).

Robert A. Johnson, We, Understanding the Psychology of Romantic Love (Harper & Row, 1983)

Ann Belford Ulanov, The Feminine, In Jugian Psychology and in Christian Theology (Northwestern University Press, 1971).

Deborah Tannen, You Just Don't Understand (Harper, 1990).

John A. Sanford, The Invisible Partners, How the Male and Female in Each of Us Affects Our Relationships (Paulist Press, 1980).

Richard Rohr with Joseph Martos, From Wild Man to Wise Man, Reflections on Male

Spirituality (Franciscan Media, 2005)

Edward C. Whitmont, The Symbolic Quest, Basic Concepts of Analytical Psychology

(Princeton University Press, 1991)

Robert B. Ewen, An Introduction To Theories of Personality, 7th Edition (Psychology Press, 2010)

Alice von Hildebrand, The Privilege of Being a Woman (Sapientia Press, 2002).

William Bridges, Transitions, Making Sense of Life's Changes (Da Capo Press, 2004).

Editors of Men's Health Books, Why Does He Do That?!, Why Does She Do That?! (Rodale Press, 1998).

James Martin, S.J., The Jesuit Guide to (Almost) Anything (Harper One, 2010).

Charles J. Healey, S.J., Christian Spirituality, An Introduction to the Heritage (St. Pauls, 1999).

J. Brian Bransfield, Living the Beatitudes (Pauline Books & Media, 2011).

Wilkie Au and Noreen Cannon, Urgings of the Heart (Paulist Press, 1995).

Dean Brackley, The Call to Discernment in Troubled Times, New Perspectives on the Transformative Wisdom of Ignatius of Loyola (Crossroad Publishing Co., 2004).

Ronald Rolheiser, The Shattered Lantern, Rediscovering A Felt Presence of God (Crossroad Publishing Co., 2004).

Richard Rohr, Things Hidden, Scripture as Spirituality (St. Anthony Messenger Press, 2008).

Raniero Cantalamessa, OFM CAP, Contemplating the Trinity, The Path to the Abundant Christian Life (The Word Among Us Press, 2007).

Federico Suarez, Mary of Nazareth (Scepter, 2003).

Robert W. Spruce and Sherri C. Southers, A Journey of A New Person, Harden Not Your Heart (Second Edition, Next Century Publishing, 2018).

REFERENCES

CCC 1605: Holy Scripture affirms that man and woman were created for one another…The woman, "flesh of his flesh", his equal, his nearest in all things, is given to him by God as a "helpmate"; she thus represents God from who all wisdom comes out help.

CCC 369: Man and woman have been created, which is to say, willed by God: on the one hand, in perfect equality as human persons: on the other in their respective beings as man and woman….Man and woman are both with one and the same dignity "in the image of God."

CCC 733: God is Love"[124] and love is his first gift, containing all others. "God's love has been poured into our hearts through the Holy Spirit who has been given to us.

CCC 1609 In his mercy God has not forsaken sinful man. The punishments consequent upon sin, "pain in childbearing" and toil "in the sweat of your brow," also embody remedies that limit the damaging effects of sin. After the fall, marriage helps to overcome self-absorption, egoism, pursuit of one's own pleasure, and to open oneself to the other, to mutual aid and to self-giving.

CCC 1850: Sin is an offense against God: "Against you, you alone, have I sinned, and done that which is evil in your sight."[122] Sin sets itself against God's love for us and turns our hearts away from it. Like the first sin, it is disobedience, a revolt against God through the will to become "like gods,"[123] knowing and determining good and evil. Sin is thus "love of oneself even to contempt of God."[124] In this proud self- exaltation, sin is diametrically opposed to the obedience of Jesus, which achieves our salvation.[125]

CCC400: The harmony in which they had found themselves, thanks to original justice, is now destroyed: the control of the soul's spiritual faculties over the body is shattered; the union of man and woman becomes subject to tensions, their relations henceforth marked by lust and domination.[282] Harmony with creation is broken: visible creation has become alien and hostile to man.[283] Because of man, creation is now subject "to its bondage to decay".[284] Finally, the consequence explicitly foretold for this disobedience will come true: man will "return to the ground",[285] for out of it he was taken. Death makes its entrance into human history.[28]

"The Christ in You", Alana Levandoski, Christian & Gospel, 20-15.

ABOUT THE AUTHORS

Robert (Bob) W. Spruce:

Bob has always been active in the Christian community becoming Catholic at the age of 50. He is certified as a Spiritual Director in his Diocese, active in prison ministry and the ACTS Retreat community, and is a lay member of the Society of Mary (religious order). He has a degree in Theology from an Episcopal seminary and has a degree in International Economics from the School of International Service at The American University and an M.B.A. in International Business from American.

Bob retired from the Unisys Corporation after 33 years and formed a family business, S&S Texas Properties, LLC in 2009. With Sherri Bob formed SR Friends, Inc. in 2009 to write books and other authored works associated with Christian spiritual relationships and spiritual friendship.

He resides in The Woodlands, Texas, is married with 3 children and 7 grandchildren.

Sherri C. Southers:

Sherri C Southers is an active Certified Spiritual Director within the Catholic Diocese of Galveston-Houston, Texas. One of her deepest desires is to companion individuals on their journey with God. She was instrumental in the implementation and development of the Cornerstone Catholic Bible Study within her home parish and remains an active member in this community. She has served on the Women's ACTS

Team as the Spiritual Director ministering to the team members and offering spiritual direction to those who attended the retreat. Sherri has written various reflections for each community, presented them to various groups and has lead group retreats. She has a B.A. in English from the University of Houston-Victoria.

www.ingramcontent.com/pod-product-compliance
Ingram Content Group UK Ltd.
Pitfield, Milton Keynes, MK11 3LW, UK
UKHW022226230426
12048UKWH00016BA/1085